Other Books by Lee Ezell

The Missing Piece
The Cinderella Syndrome
Private Obsessions

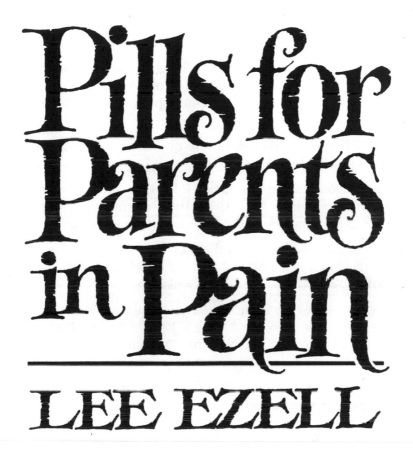

Pills for Parents in Pain

LEE EZELL

WORD PUBLISHING
Dallas·London·Vancouver·Melbourne

PILLS FOR PARENTS IN PAIN

Unless otherwise marked, Scripture quotations are from the King James Version of the Bible.

Those marked NIV are from The Holy Bible, New International Version. Copyright © 1973, 1978, 1984 International Bible Society. Used by permission of Zondervan Bible Publishers.

Those marked NASB are from the New American Standard Bible © 1960, 1962, 1963, 1968, 1971, 1972, 1973, 1975, 1955 by The Lockman Foundation. Used by permission.

Those marked RSV are from The Revised Standard Version of The Bible, copyright 1946, 1952, © 1971, 1973 by the Division of Christian Education of the National Council of the Churches of Christ in the U.S.A., and are used by permission.

Those marked TLB are from The Living Bible, copyright © 1971 by Tyndale House Publishers.

Library of Congress Cataloging-in-Publication Data:

Ezell, Lee
    Pills for parents in pain : prescriptions of hope for the headaches & heartaches of parenting / Lee Ezell
    p. cm.
    ISBN 0–8499–3385–4
    1. Parenting—United States.   2. Parenting—Religious aspects—Christianity.   I. Title.
HQ755.8.E99   1992
649'.1—dc20
    92–21691
    CIP

3 4 5 9 LB 9 8 7 6 5 4 3 2

Printed in the United States of America

Contents

DEDICATION

to Edna Ezell,
with gratitude and love:
my surrogate mother,
and my painless mother-in-law

Foreword

When I was a teen-ager, I remember thinking, "My parents are so good. How do they always know the right thing to do—when to bless, when to confront, when to be serious, when to have fun?" I was in awe of the whole parenting process and its complications as well as its great joys.

When I held our first child, Suzanne, in my arms I remember asking myself, "How will I know when to encourage, how to discipline, when to laugh, and how to affirm?" Again, I was overwhelmed with the awesome and glorious mandate to parent a real child with an eternal soul.

Now that our children are all through college and on their way to being adult contributors to the lives of others, Bill and I are beginning to wonder if maybe those three didn't teach us much more than we taught them. At least we are coming to believe that—more than our being responsible to each other and to God—we are all, today and always, "kids under construction."

In an age of parent-bashing, child-hating, elder-discarding, and family-disparaging, it is a breath of fresh air to find Lee Ezell's realistic and biblical encouragement of individuals. A large proportion of individuals were not parented perfectly, nor have they perfectly parented their own children. The accompanying guilt, shame, disappointment, and despair can keep us blind and paralyzed to the good things God has for families—things like healing, hope, and, on a given day, a little bit of heaven!

Gloria L. Gaither

Introduction

My dear parent, nobody knows better than I do that you deserve a break today. I understand your need; I signed up for Low Impact Parenting, but wound up in an exhausting Aerobic Parenting Workout! In the following pages, I hope we can work together to cope with our feelings of fatigue, frustration, and perhaps even failure as parents.

This book is offered to you as a pain reliever, to encourage you, and help alleviate your parenting distress. Of course, my words don't come to you from a clinical standpoint—there are plenty of books like that around. Although we may borrow some insights from the experts, we'll leave the discipline, training, and family development instructions to Dr. Dobson and the rest of the child psychologists (bless them all—what would we do without them?).

Instead, this is my official, practical, "in-the-trenches" perspective, which I write both as a parent and a stepparent.

- You are about to digest some megavitamins for that extra boost you need.
- You'll receive special shots in the arm for sagging spirits.
- You'll be comforted by a balm of encouragement to soothe your broken heart.
- You will be offered some preventive therapy, too, to help avoid future despair.

I write based on my own life's experience, years of counseling with parents about their various dilemmas, and some of my favorite biblical principles. I sincerely hope that a deeply healing experience awaits you.

The following is offered for every parent—whether you are a birth parent, stepparent, or adoptive parent; whether your parenting experience finds you single, or sharing your responsibilities with a spouse. Rather than another technical book on *How to Raise a Successful Child,* think of this as *How to Successfully Survive the Parenting Experience.*

It's all but impossible never to feel a twinge of regret in the throes of parenting; it's as impossible as making birth control retroactive! Still, most of us did our best, or are still in the process of trying. And even when we've failed ourselves or our children, God remains faithful in offering forgiveness and support.

We have words of encouragement for parents whose emotional climate is *not* "fair and mild," and who have reason to fear that a hurricane is forming off their coast. Some of us are parents with problem rascals of preschool or grade-school age. Some are struggling with moody adolescents, or with the prodigal syndrome. Still others have "boomerang kids" who keep returning home. Let's remind ourselves that it is not possible for anyone to raise the same child for eighteen years; our precious boys and girls don't *stay* the same for eighteen years.

Reading this book is no guarantee that you'll be healed by the last chapter. But, as a mom who made many mistakes, I know sharing the pain of others does ease our own distress. Most important of all, I hope my words serve to remind you that the Great Physician can perform a miraculous transplant—He can provide you with a new heart, filled with hope for the future.

1

Parents in Pain

Common Symptoms

IT'S MOTHER'S DAY. IF THE CHILDREN are still at home, one of them may bring you breakfast in bed (beware the scalding coffee and the rock-hard toast, and bear in mind that it's the thought that counts). A handful of limp dandelions probably decorates your TV tray, along with a folded paper towel bearing the words "I love you, Mommy" carefully printed in red crayon.

If your offspring are grown up and have moved out, they may meet you at church, hoping to please you with their spirituality. They'll doze through the service, take you to a restaurant and present you with yet another bottle of the perfume you wore when they were ten years old. (How can you bring yourself to tell them that you stopped wearing it decades ago?) The fact is, these kinds of loving gestures are only for lucky Moms—the mothers who are still being honored by their offspring.

Some mothers' stories are far different. One friend of mine sat alone last year, without so much as a phone call or a card, because her daughter's therapist had advised her that she needed "time out" from her mom. "Time out from what?" the poor woman asked herself all day. "Does mothering have the same rules as basketball?"

Another acquaintance of ours spends Mother's Day year after year in her retirement complex, with two $29.95 florist's bouquets on display, one sent from each of her two children. Although they live less than two hours away from her, even Mom's special day doesn't inspire a personal visit. They have apparently taken the advertising admonition "Say it with flowers" a little too seriously.

Second Thoughts

Whether it's Mother's Day or not, on some occasion or another we may all find ourselves mulling over one lingering thought, "Where did I go wrong?" Let's face it— the days of families like the Brady Bunch, the Partridges, and the Nelsons are over! We are now "Married with Children"; many a "Dr. Huxtable" has failed (Father doesn't always know best . . .), and we still have Bart Simpson at home!

I can remember moments when I desperately wanted to hang a sign on the back of my teen-agers' doors, a sign that read, "Checkout Time Is 18." Or, maybe this one would have been even better:

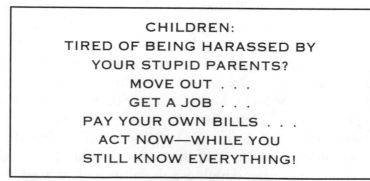

```
CHILDREN:
TIRED OF BEING HARASSED BY
YOUR STUPID PARENTS?
MOVE OUT . . .
GET A JOB . . .
PAY YOUR OWN BILLS . . .
ACT NOW—WHILE YOU
STILL KNOW EVERYTHING!
```

But when is the parent's checkout time? When do we clock out as parents? The answer, of course, is never. We are always on duty, on call, on the spot, and maybe even teetering on the edge. Where did I get the idea that I had only a few years to go, that our kids' eighteenth birthday was always just around the corner? Of course now some of us look back fondly at eighteen. Those were the good old days!

One night my husband Hal and I were moderating a support group for parents in pain. After we closed the final meeting, a large handsome fellow approached us. His body was bristling with fitness (I couldn't help but notice); later we identified him as a linebacker for the Los Angeles Rams. This distressed dad expressed his disappointment and pain over his two sons.

"I'm struggling with thoughts like, 'Where did I go wrong . . . Why do they act this way . . . How soon will this pass?'" I shook my head sadly, wondering exactly what he was dealing with. Promiscuity? Belligerence? Cocaine addiction?

With a sympathetic smile, I inquired, "How old are your sons"?

"Five and seven," he sighed wearily.

Hal and I glanced at each other in disbelief. We didn't have the heart to tell him (even in Christian love), "Oh, buddy, you've only just begun!"

It reminded me of a colorful ad that had once caught my eye:

> Experience a Dramatic Improvement in
> Your Child's Behavior!
> Listen to 1–2–3 Magic Tapes that will
> transform your home!
> No arguments. No anger.
> Just results.

Hope was just beginning to dawn in my heart when I happened to catch the fine print—"Ages 2 to 12." Unfortunately, my kids were too old for magic, at least for that kind of enchantment. They had already entered the "Kodak generation"—they were overexposed and underdeveloped teens.

The truth of the matter is this: there are no age limits on parental pain, either for parents or kids. We never outgrow it; it never outdistances us. Mothers, in particular, seem to have a deeply-rooted intuition that simply says, Something's about to go wrong; something is wrong; or something awful has just happened. This peculiarity is as unremovable as our hearts themselves.

Playing the Blame Game

It is often in the wake of those "things that went wrong" that parents ask themselves the unanswerable questions:

"Why, God?"

"What if? . . . How come? . . . Why me?"

"Where did I blow it?"

Parents who struggle with strong-willed or rebellious children are particularly inclined to believe that they most certainly have failed somewhere. These mothers and fathers have been through thousands of power struggles. They have tried countless forms of discipline, and frequently have concluded that not a single one of them works. They've believed (secretly or not) the worst of their child, anticipating such dreadful outcomes as jail sentences, numerous unplanned pregnancies, and ongoing substance abuses. Sad to say, some of them have lived to see their worst fears realized. Then begins the process I call the Blame Game. We blame:

- That insensitive, uncooperative second-grade teacher
- The church youth program

- The neighbor kids and their lousy influence
- The boss that made us work too many hours
- The company that made us move too many times
- The spouse that never seemed to care as much as we did

Cathy is the kind of mother who breast-fed her infants until they were nearly old enough to make sandwiches for themselves. She prepared organic baby food in the food processor, and never even allowed a baby-sitter on the premises until Justin and Carrie were three and four years old, respectively.

Carrie, her blond-haired, brown-eyed daughter always was an angel, gentle and peaceable as her kind-hearted mother. Justin, however, was quite another matter. From the day of his birth, he bellowed, roared, thrashed around, and glared. Once he was able to talk, he added verbal insults to his collection of control weapons. Poor Cathy hated confrontations even more than she hated Justin's outbursts. Meanwhile, Jim, her husband, was so similar in temperament to Justin (or vice versa) that their conflicts were explosive and frightening. Sometimes Jim's idea of corporal punishment verged all-too-close to physical abuse.

As Justin developed, the terrible twos became the terrible threes, soon followed by the terrible fours, fives, and sixes. Psychologists were consulted, tests were administered, schoolteachers were briefed, but all to no avail.

Carrie remains an angel to this day. Justin, now in his terrible teens, has already had several encounters with the local police. He has been expelled from private school, suspended from public school, and Cathy and Jim are seriously considering a boarding school as a possible solution. When you ask Cathy about Carrie, she smiles. When you

ask her about Justin, she sighs and rolls her eyes in resignation.

Who is really to blame for Justin's problems? Only God
knows.

As often as not, a parent in pain has been a highly
motivated mother or father, who, like Cathy, welcomed
child-rearing responsibilities with enthusiasm. They are often educated, middle-class people who once shared an ide-
alistic outlook about family life.

If you are a parent feeling pain, you probably qualify
as being among the most committed, steadfast, devoted of
parents. We shouldn't wonder why we find ourselves struggling so intensely with our parenting discomfort. We hurt
to the same extent that we love.

And we love very, very much.

Like Parent, Like Child

> **MENTAL ILLNESS IS HEREDITARY**
> **YOU GET IT FROM YOUR KIDS**

Does this sound vaguely familiar to you? "You'll be
sorry—you'll have kids of your own someday."

That's right—it's your mother speaking. Or your father. Or, worse yet, both of them talking at the same time,
glaring at you across the dining room table. "I hope you
remember someday how you've made us feel. I hope your
kids hurt you the way you've hurt us!"

We cringe at these echoing words. Are they some kind
of spooky parental prophecy coming to pass before our very
eyes? Are we finally reaping what we sowed all those years
ago? A quick inventory of past incidents may not exactly
comfort us as we recall our own crass and cavalier conduct.

Every frustrated mother (or father) reaches into her
own growing-up experiences for possible explanations. But

a parent in pain is not living out the results of a hex or curse cast upon you during some past bewitching experience. Too many parents, now in pain, were model children, who never gave their own moms and dads more than a moment's difficulty. Still, a look back may well be in order. How did the way our parents raised us influence us as adults?

Considering the kind of role modeling my parents provided, I could only assume that my own children would grow up to wear ski masks over their faces and rob convenience stores. If I had been fluent in today's psychobabble, I would have described my growing up like this:

"I am a co-dependent adult child of an alcohol, in recovery from a dysfunctional family, and my inner child was apparently adopted out."

My own mother is still alive; although she is quite feeble, I remember her as strong, the thirty-year wife of a violent alcoholic. Mother built a shield around herself for protection from the emotional wounds her husband inflicted on her. But her "Great Wall" also kept all five of her children at an uncomfortable distance. Being open and vulnerable was much too risky; besides, her own drinking problem protected her from intimate communication.

Mother's armor, as the years rolled by, became impenetrable. This, coupled with her German heritage made her a veritable fortress. There was rarely an expression of caring in our home. We only exercised defensive survival tactics.

My earliest childhood memories are of the family running for cover as my crazed father climbed the steps from his dismal basement dwelling. After physical abuse, screams and cries, one of us would make it to the phone to call the police for help. Language was vile, and tempers ran hot in our household. That tragic scenario was continuously repeated in our home, which was located deep in Philadelphia's inner city.

I was a rather compliant child. Fear of retribution will do that to you. But a developing sense of humor and a forthcoming spiritual experience instilled the hope in me that, no matter how unpleasant things got with my parents, my own future family didn't have to follow suit.

Assurance that my past could be left behind came when I stumbled upon a religious meeting and heard something that was all new to me. The preacher's name was Billy Graham, and his words introduced me to a new Friend who would willingly share my struggles and heartaches. That night of simple surrender to Christ convinced me that I was no longer alone. At last I had a real Father, and I was willing to try and trust Him for the parenting I needed.

Pain from the Past

But the healing of the effects of the past is not an overnight, instant happening; there is no God-magic. God is not a fairy godfather who says, "Bibbidi-bobbidi-boo," and all the past is magically erased. Instead, with skill and all the time in the world, He begins the re-parenting operation. And, unfortunately, there aren't many of us who don't need this. In America today, 94 percent of us report that we came from "dysfunctional homes," so only 6 percent of us got all we needed from our earthly parents.

I'm quite sure that the restoring-of-my-soul process began with my willingness to forgive. My parents were the first names on a long list written on my yellow legal pad—a personal inventory of people that I very much needed to pardon. I believe that the process of forgiveness, as Karen Burton Mains puts it, "is well worth the effort it takes to yank our wills to that painful point of obedience." Our job is to accept God's role as Father in our lives and receive His forgiveness (as we forgive our parents who have trespassed against us). Then the doors to emotional healing can swing open and the process can begin—for all of us!

There are certain "personal evangelists" who have a habit of greeting potential converts with the words, "Did you know God loves you and has a wonderful plan for your life?" Well don't laugh—because, as a matter of fact, it is true! God does have a wonderful plan for each us, and He wants to bring that plan to pass—regardless of our inadequate parental experiences, past abuses, or unhealthy role models. The Bible is clear about God's strategy:

> For I know the plans I have for you; . . . they are plans for good and not for evil, to give you a future and a hope.
> Jeremiah 29:11 TLB

God guarantees the validity of His parenting role to us in Matt. 7:11. He asks if we, as earthly parents, know how to "give good gifts" to our children, how much more will He, as our heavenly Father, give us everything we need?

As we look back, we can diagnose unhealthy patterns we may have learned from our childhood home life. As we look at the present, we may need to prescribe for ourselves a strong dose of forgiveness—of our parents, of ourselves, of our sons and daughters. As we look toward the future, we can enjoy the tonic of hope—hope in God's "good plan," an elixir of confidence that He is able, more than able, to bring about things in our lives that are better than we could ask or think!

Pain from Parental Burnout

"Parent burnout" is one of the newly identified stresses of the nineties. As many as 50 percent of parents will experience at least the early stages of burnout. And it is the most sincere, dedicated parents who suffer this emotionally malignant condition most critically. Has your "protective ozone layer" been burned off by adolescent pollution and developmental toxic waste? See if you can identify with any of these stages of parental burnout.

1. *Enthusiastic Stage.* These wide-eyed, eager parents believe that they are indispensable to their children's happiness. Parenting is literally their whole life. They drop many activities to focus total attention on their kids. With expectations high and energy unflagging, they tackle the parenting challenge.

2. *Doubting Stage.* Noticing disturbing trends and attitudes, these parents have a growing sense that they are doing something wrong. Moms and dads quickly come to the conclusion that their poor attempts at parenting have created the moods, miseries, and mayhem that suddenly seem to surround them. Parents in the doubting mode may begin to feel guilt pangs and should avoid unwholesome "painkillers" that amount to addictive behaviors.

3. *Overwhelmed and Retreating Stage.* This parent feels tied to a relentless daily schedule of pacifying an ungrateful child. By now, unrealized high expectations have plummeted into feelings of futile sacrifice and martyrdom. Financially, the family motto becomes: "Parents maketh; kids taketh." The overwhelmed parent begins to dislike the child, and may even develop a sort of paranoia—"he's just doing this for spite."

4. *Disenfranchised Stage.* Disenchanted parents feel like giving up—throwing in the towel, resigning. They

isolate themselves from the support of others, feeling trapped and hopeless. Self-doubts take over, and parents in this state of mind begin to question their value system—"I just should have let my kids run wild like Mrs. Wilson from across the street did. Her kids are no worse than mine."

Are you approaching burnout? Recognize the fact that you may be struggling with burnout simply because you have a value system which is worth fighting for. True, you may have fought too hard. Or you may not have battled as courageously as you might have wished. And it may be that you are still in the midst of the struggle, farther from your original high expectations than you would have hoped.

One thing is sure, you need some support. You are definitely not alone, no matter what your circumstances. Human comfort is helpful and necessary. And you shouldn't feel that God has turned His back on you, either. He's there, whether you're aware of His presence or not. Turn to Him, persistently and boldly. And remember—God is in control. His timing is perfect. And He doesn't make mistakes.

Thresholds of Pain

Meanwhile, during the time you're waiting on Him, why not have some fun? Enjoy life. Take time for your friends. Watch a funny movie. And read an uplifting book (like the rest of this one, for example).

Some parents are still entrenched in the endless efforts required by toddlers. Others are trying to survive with the "can you help me with my homework?" generation. Still others are watching the clock, marking the calendar, mentally turning Junior's black-hole-of-a-bedroom into a fragrant, romantic Laura Ashley-inspired guest accommodation.

The problem with kids is that they are here today . . . and here tomorrow. But even after they pack, kiss you goodbye and drive into the horizon, grief can still linger. Reminders of the problem child remain—the intersection where the accident occurred, the dents in the walls, the cigarette burns in the furniture.

Each parent has a different pain threshold. One parent may be crushed because his child cheated in school; another may be devastated that her son has long hair. Someone may be dreading the upcoming moment when a daughter moves in with her boyfriend; someone else is wholeheartedly wishing that a lesbian daughter would find a nice boyfriend to move in with! No matter how much worse another parent's troubles may be, they certainly don't *feel* any worse than you do. Many a parent could wear a medical warning bracelet:

> **I'M SUFFERING FROM
> A SEXUALLY TRANSMITTED
> DISEASE . . .
> CHILDREN!**

Of course, some mothers and fathers are faced with difficulties that have afflicted their children's lives through no one's fault. Some youngsters are hindered by the residual effects of accidents, diseases, birth defects, or broken relationships. When a child like that has heartaches, the parents share his sorrow. And, with all children, no matter who's to blame, parents remain connected to their offspring, whether they want to be or not.

Pain—Outside and Inside

The agonies we parents experience over our children's troubles are intensely real. And besides their ongoing escapades, we've got plenty of problems to deal with ourselves:

Our unforgiveness
Our withdrawal
Our anger
Our feelings of intimidation
Our disappointment
Our shame
Our resentment
Our humiliation

It may seem easier *not* to deal with these things now. After all, we already have enough on our hands with a wayward or wounded child. You may find *yourself* wanting to run away from home. I know I've packed my own bags more than once.

Wanda, an attractive single parent, tearfully recounted the conflicting emotions she experienced while attending a mother-daughter brunch at her local church.

"I tried to sit there and look interested," Wanda admitted, "as this pompous woman lined up her offspring and began her boasting. 'This is my oldest girl, Sheila. She and her plastic surgeon husband volunteer time overseas to care for needy and disadvantaged children. Here's my precious number-two daughter; Bonnie Jean is a pastor's wife. And here's our youngest one, Vonda Lee, who's finishing up her Bible school training, getting herself ready to go the Black Snake River and help in the leper colony . . . I'm just so proud!'"

Wanda continued, "While I was wiping away my own tears and trying to be happy for her, I was looking for a place to hide. What if they asked me about my own kids? I'd have to say, "Oh, I'm so glad you asked. The oldest daughter is living in Chicago with her boyfriend, supporting him through acting school. They tell me I may soon be a grandmother. . . . My son is just finishing up another stay at an alcohol rehab center . . . our other daughter is finalizing her divorce. My ex-husband and his new wife (the one who used to be his secretary) are helping her with the legal part. I just feel so proud. . . ."

Sometimes Christian social settings are the most painful places of all for parents in pain. It shouldn't be that way—God has more than His share of prodigals running around the globe—but it is.

In certain Christian circles where the Word of God is held sacred, there are always individuals who delight in finding out just who is obeying that sacred Word and who isn't. These people have been around ever since there were Scriptures to obey, and they are able to influence the attitude of an entire congregation when they sit in powerful church positions.

These people even have a scriptural explanation for their nosiness. They'll tell you, "The Lord says 'by their fruits you shall know them,' and I'm one of His fruit inspectors." You and your children might well have come under the judgmental eye (and word!) of such individuals, causing you to feel a great sense of humiliation.

Pain That Persists

When we feel alienated from fellow believers because they simply cannot share our plight, we may be tempted to feel alienated from God, too. In my own times of difficulty, I must admit that my own faith has been stretched almost to the breaking point. In those times I know very well that God is aware of our painful parenting situation, but at times He seems uninvolved.

I know I should hope for the best, but I imagine the worst. I know the Bible says, "fret not thyself," but as a parent, I'm a world-class fretter. Let me describe for you some of the feelings I've had. Maybe they'll sound familiar to you.

During parenting problems, all the things I think I "know" about God's healing power don't ease my pain. When I glance over at a picture of my laughing child on a little tricycle, tears flood my eyes. It was all so sweet and hopeful when they were young. Why do things have to change? Why does life have to be so difficult?

Questions thunder across my mind. Did I do enough as a mother? Did I do too much? Am I hindering my child? Or enabling her? What is my part? What is hers? Volunteering for parenthood is like requesting that a bowling alley be installed in your head!

Although I feel as if I'm trusting God, I'm losing confidence in myself. Wouldn't a better parenting job have produced a better child? Will my child sting me with the guilt of having produced a "dysfunctional family"? Will I be the next "Mommie Dearest"?

I've tried praying, but somehow it doesn't feel as if my words are getting through to anybody. And why do I feel so apprehensive? Am I torturing myself needlessly, or is God giving me discernment? Am I just suspicious, or perceptive?

I ache from disappointment for what might have been. I'm wounded from trying to hug a porcupine-child. I grieve for the hope I've lost for this child—I mourn the loss of that hope.

Most important of all, I ask if our relationship can be restored. Will this parent in pain ever be healed? These questions, of course, should be answered: Yes! Yes! And, in case you're afraid to ask, no, this is not a terminal condition we're talking about.

Christian Parents' Unique Pain

Christian parents really do have more reason than others to be hopeful about their children's ultimate peace of mind. But they sometimes experience a particular and specific kind of pain, and this pain emanates from an investment of their personal faith in their children's lives. They feel the anguish of trying to be loving and lovable parents while bringing up their children in accordance with a very real moral and spiritual commitment.

As the beautician washed out my hair, she continued bragging about her two daughters. They were so close, "such dolls"!

Later, they appeared in the shop to hug mom and take her out for lunch. While they were there, I overheard them laughing together about Mom taking them (underage) to a male stripper joint. Mom was so rad—so totally awesome. Because of this irresponsible parenting, these daughters just loved to hang out with their mom. At the same time you'll find morally upright parents who are trying their best, teaching sound principles, and being good examples. And for that very reason they are estranged from their rebellious and disrespectful kids.

While a non-Christian parent may seem more relaxed at parenting, the spiritually-oriented parent marches to a different drummer. Our family values and moral principles are not up for grabs; we never view the Ten Commandments as multiple choice options.

At times, Christian parents are perceived as not as "cool," not nearly as "understanding," and certainly not as "easy-going" as their secular counterparts—my hair-stylist friend, for example. While some parents may adjust their standards in accordance with what is socially acceptable, other parents refuse to compromise on the vital issues. For most Christians, situation ethics are as unacceptable as the bad situations they often cause.

It is tough for the concerned parent simply to smile and murmur, "He seems like a neat guy," when your son brings home a flamboyantly homosexual friend. And when a beloved daughter's boyfriend wants to take her away alone for the weekend, we are simply unable to answer, "Great idea! Have a terrific time and don't forget the condoms." Moms and dads with strong religious values are not as permissive or indulgent as other parents whose ethical standards change with each new issue of *Self, Cosmopolitan,* or *G.Q.*

Several things must be kept in mind when our personal spiritual life contributes to our struggles as a parent. For one thing, God will honor our efforts to instill His values in the hearts of our sons and daughters. For another, we are not supposed to be judge and jury of our children's every action—we are simply to show them the right way and explain the reasons for our chosen path. The rest is up to them.

By now it's quite obvious that parental pain springs from a number of sources. Some of it is unnecessary. Some of it is unavoidable. But whatever your source of pain may be, whether from past wounds, heartaches about the future, or headaches about the present, there is relief waiting for you! The following checklist for parents will help you properly diagnose the cause of your parental pain.

Checklist for Parents in Pain

This questionnaire will help identify some beliefs that underline your feelings as a parent. Mark each statement that applies to you.

____ I am responsible for my child's behavior.

____ I have nobody to blame but myself.

____ It is up to me to make my child happy.

____ I want my child to be my pride and joy.

____ I can't tell my child how much he/she hurts me.

___ I shouldn't do anything that would hurt my child's feelings.

___ I suspect my child feels we are a dysfunctional family.

___ My child's feelings are more important than mine.

___ I often give in to my child, no matter how I feel.

___ I often pretend things are alright when they are not.

___ I am trying very hard to change my child.

___ It's my fault that we argue so much.

___ If my child would change, I would feel better about myself.

___ I feel guilty when my child is punished.

___ I feel guilty when I do something that upsets my child.

___ I feel guilty about my anger toward my child.

___ I feel guilty when I say "no" to my child.

___ I feel scared when my child is angry at me.

___ I feel sad when my child is unhappy.

___ I feel I've let my child down.

___ I feel ashamed about my child.

___ I feel my child is ruining my life.

___ I'm disappointed in myself that I couldn't make life better for my child.

If five or more statements were checked, you are totally enmeshed with your child. You should begin to recognize that your beliefs are self-defeating and may be preventing you from being a separate, independent person as well as a parent. These beliefs can increase your dependency on your own children, and can aggravate the tension which hangs suspended between you.

But don't be discouraged. Rejoice! There's help available whether you need intensive care or just a little first aid now and then. The Great Physician is on duty, the Wonderful Counselor makes house calls, and the Heavenly Father is willing to share His parenting wisdom with everyone who'll listen.

2

Fatherly Care

An Injection of Hope

SOME FRIENDS OF MINE USED to support an underprivileged child in Guatemala for $300 a year. This needy and disadvantaged child seemed to genuinely love and admire her "wonderful American Mom and Dad." She sent pictures, shared all her activities, and expressed affection and gratitude.

After listening to a rather lengthy report about this faraway child's many virtues, I began to think, *Maybe I could send my kids to Guatemala and mail in $300—even $1,000—every year.* Would they then be more content there than with the apparently intolerable conditions they were experiencing in our home? Maybe this would make a great "child exchange program." Suppose we send our adolescents on an "adventure" for three or four years and, in their absence, temporarily adopt an equal number of adorable, grateful youngsters who haven't yet entered the dreaded hormone zone.

Why Did God Have Children?

"Our Father, who art in heaven . . ."

I'm certainly not a theologian, but it seems to me that God became a father for the same reason the rest of us became parents: He loved. When you love, you want to share that love. For most young, married couples, a desire to share themselves with a family of their own leads to the decision to give birth to children. Perhaps these kinds of feelings reflect the fact that we are created in the image of our Heavenly Parent.

God gives spiritual birth according to the same principle: "For God so loved the world," we read in John 3:16, "that he gave his only begotten Son." What did God have in mind? He gave to "as many as received him" [Jesus] the "power to become the sons of God" (John 1:12). By receiving Jesus, God's Son, into our lives, we become "adopted" sons of God.

And how do God's sons and daughters behave toward their adoptive parent? Even though He has given both physical and spiritual birth to some of us, we have, unfortunately, given Him an immense amount of grief.

Even God, who knew the end, was willing to take a chance. He offered life, love, and provision to everyone, everywhere. But many men and women, boys and girls, even those who actually received His gifts, have broken His heart. How come God gave life when He knew there was every chance we could reject Him? Because He did not give life selfishly, solely for His own satisfaction. He wants to bless us. He wants to complete us. He wants to spend eternity with us. And for Him, it's worth the risk of rejection.

What does God want from us? He doesn't want us to behave ourselves so He can play the part of a proud father. He wants us to trust Him, because He's so much more capable than we are. And, as far as love is concerned, God the Father desires a voluntary expression of love through an act of our free will. Don't we earthly parents share this same desire? God refuses to demand affection from us, and we human parents are in a similar circumstance. We cannot control our children's affection. And just as God wants us to become everything He created us to be, we long to see our kids demonstrate a desire to change and live up to their full potential. And, of course, like God, we are required to follow His fatherly example, and to give life and love regardless of the outcome.

> ARE YOU WILLING TO ASK GOD
> TO GIVE YOU LOVE FOR A CHILD
> WHO MAY ONLY GIVE YOU PAIN IN
> RETURN?

For Better or for Worse

When most of us said our wedding vows, we did so with the understanding that the relationship was to stick together "for better or for worse." At the time, visions of true love prevailed. We couldn't imagine anything worse than washing dirty socks, fighting over the television, or being seen without make-up. It wasn't long before the rose-colored glasses slipped off our noses (as well as our spouse's) and we both began to see that "better" was something we should enjoy for all it is worth—whenever we can find it.

That same "better or worse" commitment is almost more binding in parenting than in marriage. So far, incidents of parents divorcing their children (other than by sheer abandonment) are few and far between, and one can only hope that there won't be a trend toward children divorcing their parents. But in any case, if you think that "for worse" amounts only to the worst in husband/wife relations, just try bringing up a family. I believe every marriage license should contain the following disclaimer:

WARNING! PARENTING MAY BE HAZARDOUS TO YOUR HEALTH

Parents in pain can usually be identified by worry lines which have etched themselves across the forehead, by circles the color of bruises under the eyes, and by a mouth that always seems to turn downward on the corners.

Most moms and dads will readily admit that they reveled in the prospect of children who would bring joy into their lives. They looked forward to being greeted at the door with hugs and kisses, by having a son or daughter who would return affection, share a conversation, and be an integral part of daily living. How tragic it is when the grief surrounding our children makes us almost wish that they (or we!) had never been born.

But fortunately, as always, God the Father is already way ahead of us—He's been walking this road for centuries. He gave life to many sons and daughters who have caused Him grief. An overview of church history is a sobering lesson in Christian imperfection. How His heart must have ached as He watched wars, inquisitions, atrocities, and tortures acted out—all in His name, and supposedly for His sake.

And in today's world, the picture isn't much different. When the so-called "TV evangelists scandals" began to hit the headlines, I realized I was still operating under the influence of an erroneous "Bad kid? Bad parent!" principle. Subconsciously, I found myself searching for justifications to prove to myself that those who were caught in willful sin could not truly have been born of God. But my assumption did not line up with the Biblical theology. I had to admit it; they were the Father's kids, all right. The point is, the bad behavior of the child was no reflection on the Father's efforts.

If "a bad kid is made by a bad parent" is a trustworthy rule, then God the Father must have done something outrageously wrong. Let's be honest; not all of God's children are a credit to Him. As a matter of fact, my sins may not be as newsworthy as those of some more visible transgressors, but the Bible says that when I've broken the law at any point, I've broken the whole thing. We're all in the same boat, and I'm afraid He can't refer to any of us as His "pride and joy."

Our Father Understands Our Pain

God knows this so well. He gave birth to Adam and Eve; they blew it. Then came Cain and Abel, Noah's nosy neighbors, the Babylonian Tower Construction Company, Inc. The tradition of "blowing it" was well established early in the history of the human race. And if New Testament history seems more relevant to you, consider Jesus' disloyal friend Peter, His treacherous comrade Judas Iscariot, and His early church pilferers Ananias and Sapphira.

God's people are just as prone to failure as anyone else. As the familiar slogan says, "Christians aren't perfect, just forgiven." It might be more accurate to say that Christians are anything *but* perfect, and it's only by the grace of God that we can cling to the hope of heaven!

As a parent, God understands who is responsible for His kids. He has been fully responsible *to* us, but is not responsible *for*. He has given us the right to make our own decisions. I can't picture Him nervously pacing the halls of heaven, head in hands, repeating, "Where did I go wrong? I should have put more chapters in the Bible . . . if only I'd said yes to Lee's prayer that time in Phoenix. . . ."

Yet isn't that the very way we parents act when troubles press in on us? When the kids do something inappropriate, we say, "Where did I go wrong?" If we have played a part in the problem, we need to deal with it (and we'll talk about that later), but endless self-incrimination is absurd and, in a sense, a negative ego trip. Maybe we're giving ourselves a little too much power!

Parents Who Rebel

It is possible, through dealing with all our children's struggles, that we ourselves become hardened. God often calls people to difficult tasks. Poor Ezekiel! I wouldn't want a "great commission" like his! God warned him:

> I am sending you . . . to a nation rebelling against me. . . . For they are a hardhearted, stiff-necked people. But I am sending you to give them my messages, . . . whether they listen or not . . . don't be afraid of them; don't be frightened even though their threats are sharp and barbed and sting like scorpions. Don't be dismayed by their dark scowls. For remember, they are rebels!
> Ezekiel 2:3–6 TLB

It sounds like a scene from our own households! God goes on to warn Ezekiel, as he faces these difficult ones,

> Listen . . . to what I say to you. Don't you be a rebel too!
> Ezekiel 2:8 TLB

Here is a clear warning. As parents, we can't afford to let our children's rebellion cause us to mutiny, too. Nor can we permit it to put us out of commission for service.

John, an elderly Christian statesman, told me a compelling story about his own wayward son. When John and his wife were youth pastors at a prominent church in Pennsylvania, their then–teen-age son was a disgrace to them.

He was forever in trouble with both the school and the police. And to make matters worse, he seemed to gloat at any opportunity to humiliate his mother and father in front of the church. He interrupted youth meetings with arguments. He sometimes roared by the church on his Harley Davidson motorcycle, trying to break up the services by drowning out the sermon.

One evening, after a series of ugly events had discouraged John deeply, he seriously considered quitting the ministry. Too ashamed to go on, weeping on his knees in prayer, he told God he was giving up on working with youth. How could he help others if he couldn't help his own son?

Immediately he felt impressed with words that spoke deeply into the silence of his heart: "John, then you won't serve Me because your son won't serve Me?"

Instantly, John understood the admonition. He was not to permit his son's rebellion to remove him from the ministry. For many years to come, the son continued to pursue his reckless and rebellious ways. But, more determined than ever, John and his wife became a most effective influence for Christ in the lives of hundreds of youth. Years later, God used John, a bona fide parent in pain, to be among the first to distribute hundreds of thousands of Bibles behind the iron and bamboo curtains. In foreign fields that spanned the globe, John inspired many thousands of young people to enter God's service.

Parenting, Solo Style

If resentment is a danger for married parents, how much more does it gnaw away at the souls of single moms and dads? Solo parenting can be a fearsome task. And sometimes the resentment extends from the children to the ex-spouse. Single parents bite their tongues in an effort not to say, "You're acting just like your father!" or "For heaven's sake, don't be like your mother when you grow up!"

And the expectations of a very demanding world sometimes create additional pressures. The fictional "Super Mom" or "Super Dad" character, composed of traits gleaned from television sitcom families, haunts the household. Single parents hold down jobs; keep house; supervise homework; chauffeur kids to sports, music lessons, and Grandma's house; cook meals; get the car serviced; go to the bank and post office; have heart-to-heart talks with their sons and daughters about major life issues; and, if they haven't lost faith along the way, they try to go to church now and then, too.

It's wise to remember that a single mom is only held responsible for being a mom; you cannot be both mom and dad. (The same is true for single fathers.) It is possible to raise healthy children in a single parent home, and survive it quite well. Many healthy and happy youngsters grow up in broken home situations; children are not necessarily warped or ruined by death or divorce.

Although church creates another demand on the parent, it's a worthwhile obligation to keep, and not only for the personal spiritual strength it provides. Children benefit from churches that furnish enjoyable activities, a wholesome peer group, and respectable role models. And as we consider the provision God has made for single-parent families through the church, we should also remind ourselves of the special promises He has specifically made to each and every single mom.

- God has committed Himself to be her husband.

     For your Maker is your husband—the LORD Almighty is his name. . . . The LORD will call you back as if you were a wife deserted and distressed in

spirit—a wife who married young, only to be rejected.
. . . with deep compassion I will bring you back.
. . . with everlasting kindness I will have compassion
on you.

Isaiah 54:5–8 NIV

- God has obligated Himself to be her children's Father.

A father to the fatherless, a defender of widows,
is God in his holy dwelling. God sets the lonely in
families.

Psalm 68:5–6 NIV

- God has promised to meet all her family needs.

And my God will meet all your needs according
to his glorious riches in Christ Jesus.

Philippians 4:19 NIV

So what is your responsibility as a single parent? First
of all, try to encourage your kids to begin developing a
relationship with their heavenly Father. If the birth father
isn't everything you'd like him to be, don't place that burden on your child—keep it to yourself. And whatever you
do, Moms, don't put all your hopes on your *next* marriage
partner becoming the "father they never knew."

As Gary Richmond wrote in his excellent book *Successful Single Parenting—Going It Alone,* every single parent needs:

1. Emotional support
2. Practical help (car maintenance, balancing the checkbook, fixing the garbage disposal, etc.)
3. Rest
4. Baby-sitting
5. Money
6. Help with the child discipline

7. Adult conversation
8. Counsel for major decisions
9. Guidance on future relationships
10. Someone to "play" with (yes, you need to play)
11. Someone to cry with
12. A good listener
13. A good role model of the opposite sex for your children
14. Help reentering the job market
15. Someone to hold you and assure you that you and your children are going to be all right. (But please don't assume that this means you need to get out there and find a new mate! Whatever you do, give yourself time to heal before you jump into another male-female relationship.)

People Who Need People

Single moms and dads are not the only parents who feel the need for someone else's assistance with their child-rearing responsibilities. At times an adult friend, other than a parent, can be of immeasurable benefit to parents—a truly positive influence during the most strategic years of a child's life.

Sometimes it takes a person on the "outside" to reach the heart of a child who finds it difficult to open up to his parents. Although parents shouldn't allow themselves to become needlessly and unfairly dependent on these helpful friends, neither should we be independent of outside input. Extended family members can persuasively motivate our child for the better.

Some Christian churches make formal provision for this sort of relationship when they include spiritual mentors, or "godparents," when children first participate in church sacraments. Even when the arrangements are more casual, some individuals can be counted on to pray for your children, to love them, encourage them, and "be there" along the twisting, turning pathway toward adulthood. In our age of broken family units, blended families, and distant grandparents, what a blessing it is to include extended family members in our parenting process.

My husband and I serve in this role for a godchild, and welcome the opportunity (offered by her parents) to guide her through her difficult teen turmoils and offer a listening ear and a word of counsel. Have you located such a "significant-other" to serve as a true godparent for your difficult child? Seek and ye shall find!

A Father's Feelings

We humans are created in the image of God, and we should re-create our style of parenting after His. Often the Scriptures reveal God's heart aching over His kids. Words like grieved, anger, and displeasure are all too often found in the Bible. One particularly touching passage in the Old Testament describes His compassion for His beloved people.

> When Israel was a child, I loved him, and out of Egypt I called my son. But the more I called Israel, the further they went from me. They sacrificed to the Baals and they burned incense to images. It was I who taught Ephraim to walk, taking them by the arms; but they did not realize it was I who healed them. I led them with cords of human kindness, with ties of love; I lifted the yoke from their neck and bent down to feed them.
>
> Hosea 11:1–4 NIV

Jesus also seemed disappointed, even frustrated at times, with His own disciples. Repeatedly in the Gospels

He is recorded as saying things like, "Do you still not understand?" (Mark 8:21 NIV).

And the children He loves he chastens and disciplines, even while He is demonstrating mercy and forgiveness. We can ask the Lord to begin to instill that same capacity in us: the ability to give mercy when judgment is in order, the commitment to discipline when it is easier to be lenient.

My friend Connie called me at eleven o'clock one night. Her sons, sixteen and seventeen years old, have both been repeated guests at the local police station. That night they were "out on the town" and Connie had that familiar sinking feeling mothers get when something awful is about to happen. She asked me to pray with her. We prayed on the phone that the Lord would protect her boys and keep them out of trouble. We specifically asked that they wouldn't get drunk.

I called her the next morning, and she was as depressed as I'd ever heard her. "Lee, I can't understand it. It's as if God completely ignored our prayer."

"What do you mean? What on earth happened?"

"Well, about ten minutes after I called you, I got a call from the police department. 'Hi, Mrs. Anderson. Your kids are here.' It's so embarrassing. They've been down there so many times they're on first-name terms with the cops on night duty!"

"So, why were they there?"

"Oh, two of their friends had just bought some whiskey illegally, and they were just getting ready to share it with the boys when all four of them got busted for being underage and drinking."

"Were your guys drunk?"

"No, they hadn't even touched the stuff—the cops caught them before they could drink a drop. And for some reason they were really scared, Lee. I think they thought this was the last straw for me. . . ."

"Connie, don't you see what happened? God answered our prayer exactly the way we asked Him to!"

"What do you mean?"

"We asked for protection, and that they wouldn't get drunk. God allowed them to get arrested to warn them, and He made it happen before they got drunk and tried to drive home."

Connie was silent, and I could tell she was thinking. "You know, Lee," she finally said. "Sometimes God really does act like a father, doesn't He?"

Forgive and Forget?

Normally I'm a good, sound sleeper. But now and then worry comes along and robs me of my rest. I come by it naturally, I guess, since I was trained by one of those evasive worrywarts who classify their discomfort as "concern." In any case, I've earned my circles, bags, and wrinkles.

One problem we parents wrestle with is the instant-replay videotape library in our heads. We can reexperience—even without consciously wanting to—the night we had the big fight. The words we wish we'd never said. The time tempers flared out of control. Although God may have the capacity to bury our sins and "remember them no more," our tapes are not so easily erased.

Even if we aren't as capable of complete forgetfulness as we'd like to be, let's work on the part we do have some control over: forgiveness. Forgiving ourselves and others is an act of our will, before it can ever become a feeling. Why should we victimize ourselves, holding ourselves captive to unforgiveness? It is a far wiser decision to release those who have wronged us from our personal condemnation, and thereby open the doors to emotional healing.

I learned the power of forgiveness at a young age. As a virgin teen-ager, and a new Christian, I was raped. To make matters worse, I found myself to be pregnant as a result. I relinquished my newborn daughter for adoption, the only child I would ever bear. My very first experience with "mothering" was very painful. For years to come, I would always think of this lost daughter as "the missing piece" of my life. I could only assume that she was never to be seen again.

In actuality, the rapist victimized me the first time, but had I not forgiven him, I would have continued to be victimized by bitterness. Instead, because I was able to learn some invaluable principles from God's Word and through Christian friends, I was instead able to follow my heavenly Father's example. He is quick to forgive. He loves unconditionally. He has promised never to leave us or forsake us. Most of all He, the caring Father, gave His precious Son up for us.

God's attitude toward us is unbelievable. I love what Max Lucado wrote in *God Came Near*.

> What God did makes sense. It makes sense that Jesus would be our sacrifice because a sacrifice was needed to justify man's presence before God. It makes sense that God would use the Old Law to tutor Israel on their need for grace. It makes sense that Jesus would be our High Priest. What God did makes sense. It can be taught, charted, and put in books on systematic theology.
>
> However, why God did it is absolutely absurd. When one leaves the method and examines the motive, the carefully stacked blocks of logic begin to tumble. That type of love isn't logical; it can't be neatly outlined in a sermon or explained in a term paper. . . .
>
> Even after generations of people had spit in his face he still loved them. After a nation of chosen ones

had stripped him naked and ripped his incarnated flesh, he still died for them. And even today, after billions have chosen to prostitute themselves before pimps of power, fame, and wealth, he still waits for them.

It is inexplicable. It doesn't have a drop of logic nor a thread of rationality. Bloodstained royalty. A God with tears. A creator with a heart. God became earth's mockery to save his children. How absurd to think that such nobility would go to such poverty to share a treasure with such thankless souls.

But he did.

When we consider the enormous investment our heavenly Parent has made in us, the immense amount of forgiveness He has extended toward us, how can we do any less for those who have wronged us? Especially if they are our own children! No matter what they've done, it can't be much worse than what we've done to Him.

As John White writes in *Parents in Pain,*

> As God is to me, so must I be to my children. As he has dealt with me, so must I deal with them. Such kindness as he has shown me, such patience and forbearing, such intolerance of sin—these must I in turn show to those for whom I stand in place of God. For in my children's minds a concept of God is growing which is derived from my spouse and me, two powerful beings who gave them birth and who seem to rule over the cosmos of the home. Each time my children see a godlike attitude or action in their father or mother, the Holy Spirit will tell them, "Now you can understand a little better what your Father in heaven is like."

You may find, as you continue to read this book, that forgiveness is one of those medicines you have to take more than once. It may require a daily dose. Some of us may need to administer it to ourselves on an hourly basis. But forgiveness is really a vital emergency treatment for pain—it clears away some very unpleasant symptoms so that other remedies can be effectively applied!

3

Promises vs. Placebos

Diagnostic Mindset Corrections

SUPPOSE YOU GO TO THE DOCTOR with a headache. The doctor puts you through a series of diagnostic tests. By a process of elimination, he is able to give you some good news. First of all, you don't have a brain tumor. Also encouraging is his conclusion that your eyes aren't about to stop working, you don't have a chronic sinus infection, and blood flow to your brain isn't blocked.

That's the good news. The bad news is, you've got a problem with your back, and it's going to require several different treatments, all applied simultaneously to relieve your headaches. You'll have to take muscle relaxants. You'll require some physical therapy. From time to time you'll need a pain-relieving drug.

So far, so good. But before long you realize that your muscle relaxants make you sleepy at work. Your physical therapy sessions are leaving you with serious lower back discomfort. And your pain medicine upsets your stomach. It is quite clear that some adjustments are necessary to your prescribed treatment.

In a similar sense, if we parents are to chart a new course for our parenting in order to emerge as successful, healthy people, a slight adjustment or two in our thinking might be necessary. Let's examine our parental mindset and adjust our assumptions on some vital issues.

Adjusting Our Assumptions

A struggling father came to me with his painful parenting experiences. Overwhelmed with guilt and self-criticism, he exposed his erroneous parental assumptions:

"Well, basically I feel God gave these kids to me. I'm gonna pray and work hard at parenting, 'cause I want them to be a credit to me and to themselves. If I do my job well? They'll turn out great. But if I fail at parenting? They're gonna be failures, and then I have no one to blame but myself."

Sad to say, this dad is in the process of taking a trip into outer space with his rebellious sons, and he is sure to burn up on reentry! We can avoid a lot of pain along our parenting journey if we make a midcourse adjustment and proceed with a far more realistic and reasonable philosophy:

Mindset Adjustment

My child is simply a temporary trust from God; he is not my "property," but rather my "guest."

He is only *my* child in the sense that I am responsible to love him, train him, and discipline him.

Although I can influence him, I cannot control his behavior, and, once he's beyond early childhood, I really do not ultimately have responsibility for his decisions, either.

Therefore I cannot either boast, taking the credit, nor brood, taking the blame for my child.

I am temporarily watching over the development of this child, realizing his destiny will ultimately be decided between him and God, alone, without my help.

To sum up,

CHILDREN COME THROUGH US, NOT FROM US.

Setting this course for our parenting adventure will enable us to cope with the challenges along the way.

> A PARENT'S JOB IS TO OFFER A
> LOVING ATMOSPHERE IN WHICH
> CHILDREN CAN REBEL
> IF THEY SO CHOOSE.

Why Did We Have Children?

"I was so young," the mother painfully cried. "Our marriage was rocky from day one, and I thought having a child would solve many of our problems. I was crazy. I wanted to have a baby to bring me some happiness; someone who would love me in return. What a fool I was!"

Because of the availability of birth control methods and the social acceptability of using them (if you aren't a devout Roman Catholic), we tend to feel very much in control of the family planning process. Sometimes we become almost independent of God in this area unless, of course, there's "an accident."

But are there accidents when it comes to the birth of human beings? If the Bible is true, and I believe it is, then the decision of life is not in our hands in the first place. Whether you thought it was your idea or not, God was the one who said yes to the conception of your child, in accordance with His plan. Note these words from the Psalmist, speaking to God:

> You made all the delicate, inner parts of my body, and knit them together in my mother's womb.
> . . . You were there while I was being formed in

utter seclusion! You saw me before I was born and scheduled each day of my life before I began to breathe.

Psalm 139:13, 15–16 TLB

The Scriptures are so clear. Over and over again God reinforces the idea (for the comfort of us doubting parents!) that He was the one who decided that our children should be born. We can honestly say that our children are not our own; they are on loan from the original Owner.

**YOUR CHILD WAS
GOD'S IDEA FIRST!**

Even though a couple may decide when to *make love,* apparently God decides when to *make life!* The decision of the conception of life is not in the hands of teenagers in the back or a car, or a technician in the back of a lab. So, ultimately, the one who decided whether we had our kids "too early" or "too late" in life was God—the Father of us all.

Both Joy and Tears

If your relationship with your mother has been anything like mine, she's shed a few tears over you since your arrival on this earth. (You've probably shed a few over her, for that matter.) Do you suppose she cried when she found out she was expecting you in the first place? I have a feeling mine did! Since I was one of five children born to alcoholic parents, I'm sure my mother cried. "Such a blessing," she must have sighed, wiping her eyes. "You could die from such a blessing!"

Although some of us may have been long-awaited "bundles of joy," let's get real! Chances are there were some

mixed feelings when morning sickness hit and the realization slowly sank in. Maybe some of our mothers jumped for joy when they found out they were pregnant—with us. But not every mother-to-be says,

> Oh, this is the perfect time!
>
> This is just what I've been waiting for!
>
> None of our plans will have to change!
>
> We have plenty of money—and room—to support one more!
>
> I couldn't be happier!

Chris, a friend of mine, told me about her own tale of "family planning." Her husband hadn't wanted any children, and he was the kind of man who might well have demanded an abortion if an unexpected pregnancy had occurred. After nearly a decade of marriage, during which she was very much under his firm control, Jeff finally agreed that they could have "one child and no more."

Their first-born son was a beauty—the most adorable "Gerber" baby imaginable. He was good-looking, exceptionally intelligent, and (believe it or not) he hardly ever cried. Although my friend's husband had only grudgingly agreed to his son's birth, even he had to admit that he had a pretty nice little boy.

One day my friend was reading her Bible, and something she read impressed upon her the fact that she would be having another child. Of course she was very diligently using birth control, knowing all too well that her husband would hit the ceiling over the idea of another baby. She privately acknowledged the possibility that the Lord had spoken to her, but naturally she kept it very much to herself.

Not six weeks later, when her first son was just a year old, Chris suddenly realized that she hadn't been shopping in the female hygiene department for several weeks. Without saying a word to her husband, she raced to her gynecologist's office and took the dreaded rabbit test (for pregnancy), all the while knowing that this whole episode had something to do with God's quiet message to her.

Sure enough, as they say, "the rabbit died." Chris was in the family way again. But how would she tell Jeff? She was terrified. Would Jeff demand an abortion? She knew she could never have one, but the rift over such a major confrontation might well be irreparable.

"Oh, God," Chris moaned. "How could you let this happen to me?"

In her heart Chris heard a quiet promise. "This child will be a blessing to you."

Still, she lacked the courage to tell her husband. Should she put a note in his lunch? Leave a message on his answering machine? Write him a letter? Ask a friend to make an anonymous phone call?

As Jeff was leaving for work the day after the positive pregnancy test, Chris took a deep breath, offered up a silent prayer, and said, "Oh, by the way, there's something I need to tell you."

He looked at her uncertainly, and then at his watch. "Now? Well, hurry up, I'm late."

"Uh . . . ," she gulped.

"Well, what is it?"

The words blurted out of her mouth as if they had a mind of their own. "We're going to have another baby, but I'll talk to you about it later. I've just got to tell you one thing. I will not have an abortion! I can't. So we'll just have to work it out."

Jeff turned on his heel, his face white as a sheet. Chris slammed the door, threw herself on her bed and cried. He was cool to her for a few days, but before long the crisis passed. Months later another beautiful boy was born, this one the very image of his father.

Chris recently reported, "The first few months I was too tired to appreciate him. But it wasn't a year before I could see what a blessing he really is—he's his brother's best friend, and everybody loves him—especially Jeff. I guess God knew what He was doing, even though it didn't seem like it at the time!"

Chris's story isn't an isolated incident. Whether moms-to-be are married or single, young or old, rich or poor, there's always an adjustment to be made. Sometimes the adjustment comes after the baby is born, when the starry-eyed mother is faced with several weeks of colic or a near-terminal case of postpartum blues. But the fact remains, since children are God's idea in the first place, conceived out of His love, no matter what anyone says or thinks, there are no illegitimate children. Every baby born on this earth has a loving heavenly Father who gave it the gift of life.

As I began to apply this truth to my own circumstances, the pain of my "lost daughter" subsided. After the initial grief, I had to "let go" of her loss. Eventually this "unplanned" child was to track me down and change my life. The reunion I experienced with her after twenty years is chronicled in my book *The Missing Piece*. God is faithful!

I know from my own life's experience that what begins unexpectedly, even tragically, does not have to result in an unwanted child! My daughter Julie puts it so well, "Even though I am the product of rape, I consider myself the product of God's love. Truly it doesn't matter how I began, but what I'll become." And this is true of all of our children!

What about you? Have you been asking yourself why? Why was this child born? Why is he (or she) so difficult?

Why do I have to hurt like this over a child I never planned to have? Perhaps a new perspective is in order. We are better able to ward off the regret and remorse that can accompany difficult parenting experiences if we realize that God the Father has a plan for our children (whether they know about it or not).

Examine Your Warranty

What else has He promised us with regard to our kids? False hope is not a reliable security blanket. My sweet husband lost two wives to disease and death, and in each case he had been convinced (by well-meaning Christian friends) that those wives would be miraculously healed. People quoted all the available Scriptures to him on the subject of healing. He clung to them. He believed them. But ultimately both of these women died.

If we have a false understanding of Scripture regarding our own children, we too may be setting ourselves up for pain and disillusionment. Dashed hopes, which can spring from a misrepresentation of isolated Bible verses, may lead to frustration and discouragement.

Let me give you another personal example. For many years, because I misunderstood the verses about women in Proverbs 31, I lived beneath the shadowy feeling of being a failure as a woman. "I can't make the grade" was the feeling I got when I read those very familiar Scriptures. (I wonder how many women's brunches have used "The Proverbs 31 Woman" as a theme.) However, when you examine the context of Proverbs 31, you discover a very important point.

Look at it this way: the author of the chapter, Lemuel, had a good Jewish mother. It is very possible that the words we read there are the words of a "wannabe" mother-in-law, given to guide her son in choosing a wife.

Basically, she reflected, "Who can find a virtuous woman? They're rare as hen's teeth, Lemmie." And we're quick to agree that she was right. The class of woman Mama was talking about is not only hard to find, she's equally hard to be.

Proverbs 31 is a lofty goal, not an entrance exam for wives and fiancees. As Vickie Kraft notes in her book *The Influential Woman,*

> Before we read what the Bible says about this incredible Wife of Noble Character, let's bear in mind that her failures are not mentioned—only her successes are recorded. The Word of God shares with us the sum total of her life: the intentions of her heart, her interactions with her husband and family, and her involvement with her community. The woman's everyday frustrations are not even discussed, but you can well imagine that she had her share. . . . In any case, I don't think this passage is trying to tell us how busy we should be.

Training Up a Child

In a similar vein, it is possible that we parents have a mistaken mindset based on other Scriptures, particularly those from the book of Proverbs. We cherish the verse:

> Train up a child in the way he should go: and when he is old, he will not depart from it.
> Proverbs 22:6

Has God guaranteed the return of our prodigal children without their cooperation? Here's the dilemma. If our children don't "come back to the fold" as adults, does it mean we've not trained them up right in the first place? Let us not view this verse as God's ironclad, unconditional guarantee. If God had planned on foretelling the moral or spiritual outcome of a life, then He would not have provided every human being on earth with a free will.

Curiously, we all agree that free will is a wonderful thing—until our kids start using it against us! Yet, in spite of the obvious free-will caveat, many parents tend to count on this one verse of Scripture as a money-back, certified affirmation that, although a son or daughter may stray for a period, he (or she) ultimately is bound to return to the principles with which he was trained. And, as we've already noted, if a straying child is older, this verse becomes a condemning accusation against the parents, who obviously made a very poor stab at "training up."

As someone once told me, we parents spend the first two years training them to walk and talk. We spend the rest of our lives wishing they'd sit down and shut up!

In a more careful examination of the context of Prov. 22:6, we can readily see that it is not given as an irrevocable pledge from God. Instead, it reflects traditional Jewish thought on how family relationships usually operate. It is more of a general observation than a divine promise. The verse does not indicate, "and when they are old they will invariably—without exception—inevitably return."

Josh McDowell and Dick Day have an interesting view of that Scripture. In their book *How to Be a Hero to Your Kids,* they say,

> Unfortunately, this verse is often misunderstood by Christian parents who think it means, "Have family devotions, take children to Sunday school and church, and when they are grown up, they'll not depart from the faith."
>
> The real meaning of this verse, however, centers on that phrase "according to his way." The writer is referring to the child's way, not God's. The root

meaning of these words suggests "stimulating a desire for guidance according to one's own uniqueness."

Over in the Psalms, the same Hebrew word is translated "bend" and refers to the bending of an archer's bow. Today, with precision manufacturing, almost anyone can pick up a forty-five pound bow and do a great job of hitting the target. But in biblical days, nothing was standardized. An archer had to use his own bow and become very familiar with it. In the same way, every parent needs to know the unique characteristics of each child in the family. Training up each child in "his own way" doesn't mean you let a child run wild or allow him to get his own way all the time . . . it really means according to . . . the child's habits and interests. The instruction must take into account his individuality and inclinations and be in keeping with his physical and mental development.

Listening to Ancient Advice

The book of Proverbs is full of rich, godly advice and observations. And although, as a general rule, we are probably not intended to seek for specific promises there, we have much to gain from meditating upon this ancient book of wisdom. Reflect upon these thoughts:

- A wise son heeds his father's instruction, but a mocker does not listen to rebuke (Prov. 13:1 NIV).
- A man who loves wisdom makes his father glad, but he who keeps company with harlots, wastes his wealth (Prov. 29:3 NASB).
- Discipline your son, for in that there is hope; do not be a willing party to his death (Prov. 19:18 NIV).

- To have a fool for a son brings grief; there is
  no joy for the father of a fool (Prov. 17:21
  NIV).

It is clear from a study of Proverbs' verses about fathers and sons, that it "takes two to tango." The father is
instructed to bring up his sons properly; the son is instructed, in order to gain wisdom, to respond to parental
correction. If both parties do their part, everything will be
all right.

But what about that God-given, known-before-the-
foundation of the earth scoundrel who won't listen to anybody? Take heart, parents! On Dr. James Dobson's radio
program "Focus on the Family," the beloved child-rearing
expert noted that the proverbial "strong-willed child" out-
numbers the compliant child two to one! Yet, in a survey
Dr. Dobson cited, by the age of twenty-five years, 53 percent of these strong-willed children were returning to family values.

The "bring up a child . . ." proverb is certainly valid,
if not irrevocable. And besides, how old is "old," anyway?
Only God knows. All we parents can really do is play out
our part in training them up to the best of our ability. Their
"not departing" from the truth then becomes God's problem!

Making a Good First Impression

Some of our more liturgical churches believe in bap-
tizing infants for theological reasons they have embraced
for centuries. Meanwhile, most evangelical churches
choose to delay this sacrament until children decide for
themselves whether to participate. In those congregations
there is another tradition which takes baptism's place, and
I think it's an important one. I believe that, whether

through baptism or dedication, publicly offering our children to the Lord when they are infants does in some spiritual way "mark" them for the Master.

Do you remember the story of Hannah? She was a heartsick, childless woman who turned to God in her grief. She promised God if He would give her a son, "I will give him back to you, and he'll be yours for his entire lifetime" (1 Sam. 1:11 TLB).

After her prayer was answered and her first-born, Samuel, arrived, Hannah presented him to God by taking him to live with the high priest, Eli. Eli was to train him for the Lord's service. It's interesting to note that little Sammy's domestic situation wasn't the most conducive to godly living. Eli had two sons who led promiscuous, wanton lives, setting a terrible example for their "adoptive brother." (Apparently poor old Eli hadn't had much luck bending his own son's stubborn wills, but God used him anyway.) And, despite the terrible role models he lived with, Samuel heard the voice of God and obeyed. His faithful mother's prayers were surely following him.

Moses was similarly "branded." Although his heartbroken mother had to release her beautiful son into the waters of the Nile in the hope of saving his life, her godly "imprinting" was forever with him. After all his training to be a loyal Egyptian, at forty years of age Moses discovered his spiritual roots and went on to deliver God's people from bondage. As surely as the Jewish mark of circumcision was on Moses' physical body, so the marking of our children's hearts for Christ will influence them.

Looking Beyond the Circumstances

No matter how difficult our challenges as parents may become, we have many reasons to rejoice. First of all, our children are "loaned" to us by God, and it was His plan for our children to be born. They are His gift to bless us, and He intends for us to bless them as long as they are in our homes (even if we feel we got faulty merchandise). We also have great reserves of wisdom in God's Word which can be applied to our parenting responsibilities. And last but not least, the early "imprinting" we give our children will follow them all their lives, whether they choose the spiritual path we want them to or not.

So let's build our hope on the firm foundation of God's truth, doing the best we can as parents. And, when times get tough, let's be comforted by a heavenly Father who understands all too well the challenges of dealing with difficult children. He doesn't want us to despair in the midst of our difficulties. He wants us to see beyond them.

Charles Spurgeon sums it up well:

> The Lord's thoughts are all working toward "an expected end." God is working with a motive. All things are working together for one object: the good of those who love God. We see only the beginning. God sees the end from the beginning. He knows every letter of the Book of Providence; He sees not only what He is doing, but what will come of what He is doing.
>
> As to our present pain and grief, God sees not these things exclusively, but He sees the future joy and usefulness which will come of them. He regards not only the tearing up of the soil with the plow, but the clothing of that soil with the golden harvest. He sees the after consequences of affliction, and He accounts those painful incidents to be blessed which lead up to so much of happiness.
>
> Let us comfort ourselves with this.
>
> *Day by Day*
> *with C. H. Spurgeon*

4

Happiness Key Implants

A Pain Killer

Somehow we've got to update our thinking. After all, we are dealing with a second generation of kids raised on Dr. Spock's now-questionable theories. Remember Dr. Spock? Like the other Spock on Star Trek, he didn't breed—unbelievably, the world-famous child rearing expert had no offspring of his own. Isn't that always the way? The ones who don't have children have all the answers.

When I was single, I assumed parenting would be fun; I loved kids. Looking back, I guess I should have realized if it started with a thing called "labor," it couldn't really be all that entertaining. I still remember old wooden billboards that said, "The family that prays together stays together." I think today it might be more realistic for the sign to read,

> **THE FAMILY THAT STAYS TOGETHER
> PROBABLY ONLY HAS ONE CAR**

Without a doubt, pain is a very real part of life. But how much of our pain is unavoidable, and how much is unnecessary? Some of our pain may be the result of our own misguided refusal to accept circumstances—and people—just the way they are.

Little Jason had been naughty, and his mom sent him to his room with the admonition, "Now you go upstairs and pray to the Lord to make you a better boy!" After dragging his little body up the stairs, Jason kneeled at his bedside and reluctantly prayed; "Lord, please make me a better boy . . . but if you can't, I'm really happy the way I am."

Isn't that the problem with our kids? They're perfectly content being the way they are . . .

"I like my room messy."

"My friends think my hair looks *awesome* in a mohawk."

"I don't *feel* like talking to you."

"So I'm a C student. So what?"

"I'm an atheist, and that's the way it's going to be."

. . . and we are desperate to change them. And whether it's possible to transform another person or not, I should have received the Olympic medal for effort. As I speak before audiences around the nation, I love to see the response when I ask, "How many of you live with someone who could be a much better person if they would only listen to your advice?" I worked long and hard to change Hal. I did my very best to change my girls. But guess who had to change?

Right. *I* did.

The I-Want-to-Make-You-Happy Blues

When I married my husband Hal I got a package deal—a husband and two ready-made daughters, Sandi, who was ten years old, and Pam, who was thirteen. And as I'm sure you can imagine, not long after we were married I began to feel a lot less like Cinderella and a lot more like the Wicked Stepmother.

Both of the girls were crushed by the deaths of not one but two mothers—their birth mother and the step-mother who had cared for them from a very early age. Pam and Sandi had understandably developed a questioning attitude toward God. They couldn't accept the fact that a loving Father would have permitted their two young moms to die. They felt rejected and abandoned.

I was keenly aware that no "replacement" human being could possibly hope to make up for their loss. I knew, in spite of their uncertainty about Him and His ways, both children would have to become inextricably attached to the only One who could honestly say, "I will never leave you nor forsake you." He would have to become their Prince . . . their Savior from the injustices of life.

It didn't take too long for me to learn, however, that although I could communicate important principles like that to the girls, I couldn't make them believe. I wasn't a fairy godmother any more than I was a wicked stepmother. There was no magic wand that could magically change their minds. The choice to walk with God or away from Him was clearly theirs, and no one else on earth could make it for them.

By His grace, those two little ones who grew up under my husband's and my care are well-adjusted adults today. In the meantime, as I began to get free of my own fairy-tale thinking, I was encouraged to write my first book, *The Cinderella Syndrome*. It communicates the big lesson I learned as a new wife and a stepmom, that happiness is a choice. Here's a quote from *that* book that certainly fits *this* one.

When you hold someone else accountable for your happiness, and you wait for that person to perform, you may be setting yourself up for inevitable disappointment and disillusionment. Even the most wonderful, near-perfect person in the world will eventually let you down.

My two daughters, like many teenagers, misbehaved, disobeyed and rebelled against their parents during high school. To our dismay, they weren't turning out as we had planned! And today they won't deny that they were neither pleasant to spend time with nor the least bit lovable during those difficult years.

Part of my personal image seemed to rest on their angry young shoulders. It was hard enough trying to be a model stepmother when they were little kids. Now my entire reputation as a Christian leader was sliding down the tubes.

As I felt myself judged unfairly by our friends and fellow church members, a root of bitterness began to take root. I had trusted and relied on my daughters to perform in a manner that would make me proud and well thought of. (Wasn't I supposed to be supermom?) Instead, they were letting me down.

The problem was that my trust and reliance had been misplaced. Keeping my reputation spotless was far too big an order for my children to fill. Why is it that we parents expect our children to build parental self-esteem? I don't know but I see it happening all the time, and I have been guilty of it myself.

If I Could Change Anything About You . . .

My somewhat unique mothering circumstances have brought me to the conclusion that God never commissioned one person to change another. And there is a very good reason for that: we cannot access their wills. Have you also tried to do what the old song suggests? "Make someone happy, make just one someone happy; then you will be happy, too."

Well, I tried; but they wouldn't!

Neither you nor I can "make" a happy spouse, or a contented child. Clearly, we can contribute to their happiness (or misery). And I suppose, in a sense, we can ruin someone's day—if they allow us to. But although I can influence other people, I have no control over anyone but myself.

So why is it that when the kids are not happy, we're not happy? When they do something wrong and we punish them, they feel mad and martyred; we feel guilty and remorseful. It's an unhappy cycle, and one that needs to be broken. Why do we allow our kids to manipulate us? Why do we manipulate them?

The story is told of a naive pig farmer who wanted to breed his livestock. He corraled five female pigs, loaded them into a truck, and drove off to Pig Stud Farm. At the end of the day he asked the pig fertility expert who ran the farm how he could be sure that the breeding mission had been accomplished.

The expert, envisioning a few extra dollars in the offing, said, "It's easy, boy. If you spot 'em rolling in the grass afterward, they're content. It took. If you see 'em rolling in the mud, they're unhappy and you'd better bring 'em back."

The next day the farmer caught all the pigs in the mud. "They're unhappy, poor things," he murmured as he loaded them back into the truck and went back to the stud farm. This sad process was repeated for four days straight. Finally the farmer gave up. "I'm not going back there again—it's a waste of time and money. Just then he glanced out the window in time to see his five female pigs hoisting themselves out of the mud, smiling (as only pigs can smile), and loading themselves onto the truck.

Manipulation only works if both parties are involved in the process! And even when it does "succeed," resentment is invariably the result.

Discover Your Implant

The truth is that God has implanted a key for happiness deep down inside each one of us, in the core of our wills. No one else can access this key. Sometimes we try to give the key to others, in the hopes that they will make us happy. But somehow, they always fail. Instead, it is the power of Christ within us that can enable us to turn the key, even without the cooperation of others.

> EACH PERSON—CHILD OR ADULT—
> HOLDS THE KEY TO HIS OWN
> HAPPINESS!

This means that our kids can be happy in spite of us. And we can be happy in spite of them. No matter what our mistakes or failures, our sons and daughters can be happy, productive people because they have their own happiness key. And, when we choose to, we parents can find happiness and contentment no matter what is going on with our problem children!

> HAPPINESS IS AN INSIDE JOB!

Frankly, this holds true for all our relationships; we do not have keys for aging parents, ex-spouses, in-laws or out-laws, or close friends with their various and sundry difficulties. God has not placed our key for happiness in the pocket of any other person. How unfair that would be! Then we could always be justified in feeling like victims

of circumstances, because our key-keeper isn't cooperating with us.

How often we write mental scripts for scenes that will give us warm, fuzzy feelings. We are invariably disappointed when those scenes aren't acted out according to our scripts—the other players forget their lines, they refuse to say the right words, they don't act the way they're supposed to. In some cases, they don't even show up for the performance. Sadly, because we've placed our expectations on them instead of within ourselves, we are gravely disappointed.

God never intended that we should have to depend on other people for completion. But that doesn't mean we aren't sometimes hurt by others. At times in life we are abused. Attacked. Abandoned. That's when God's provision for our happiness comes into the picture.

In the heavenly Father's economy, the fatherless are not left fatherless. The brokenhearted are healed, not left to suffer consequences over which they had no control. Even the divorced are not left to agonize forever over their loss. Jesus was right when He said, "I will not leave you comfortless." (John 14:18). Thank God that even though pain is inevitable, misery is optional. We hold the key to our happiness. God holds the key to providing for our every need—physical, emotional, and spiritual.

The Key to Our Children's Happiness

Do you still feel like you have to make your child happy? I guess it starts when they're babies. They cry. We feed or change them. They stop crying and smile. We feel a rush of pleasure. It gets to be a habit for us to transform frowns into grins. We become quite proficient at doing so, but unfortunately, it can actually become an addictive behavior.

Maybe the kids don't know it yet, but God didn't forget to place a happiness key in their hearts. Youngsters are so vulnerable, so up and down in their emotions. They are at the mercy of their latest friend, their newest crush, or the outfit they just picked up at the mall.

"I'm bored," they moan, so Dad takes them out to play ball.

"There's nothing on this dumb TV," they complain, so Mom bakes a cake for them.

How wonderful when they begin to look *inside,* not *outside,* for their answers! Are we teaching them to do so?

Our sons and daughters will never discover true satisfaction until they begin to turn their own key to the door of happiness. Sometimes they think we parents have it. On bad days they think we've confiscated it and flushed it down the toilet. At times we all wish we had some kind of ownership of other people's happiness keys. Then we manipulate everybody else into our own way of thinking and behaving.

Living in the "Now"

Young people—in fact, many people of all ages—tend to think that happiness and contentment lie in some faraway land called "If only."

"If only I had Super Nintendo"

"If only I had a boyfriend (or a girlfriend)"

"If only I were 16 (or 18 or 21)"

"If only I had my driver's license"

"If only I had more money"

"If only I had my own car"

"If only I could go away to school"

"If only I were married"

It's important for all of us to realize that when we get lost in "If only," we are like hamsters on a treadmill. We must teach ourselves first, and then our children, to enjoy today for all it's worth. To seize the moment. To delight and be thankful for what we *do* have, and to ask God to give us whatever else we need in His time. Otherwise we are going to find ourselves bypassing life and experiencing deep disillusionment and despair.

Let's repeat these words, and have our kids repeat them after us:

"I fully realize I can't depend on you, or on anyone else, to make me happy. I can't lean on you, you can't lean on me, because neither one of us can reach any other person's happiness key."

Don't Blame Me, It's Your Fault!

Just as we may be tempted to think that we are responsible for our children's happiness, we may also find ourselves believing that we are also responsible for their behavior.

A heartsick Dad was informed that his son had been arrested for stealing. When he sat down across from his teen-ager at the police station, the son spoke angrily to his dad.

"I wouldn't have all these problems if you and Mom hadn't split up. Back then you didn't work so much, and I had more money."

Despite his sorrow over the circumstances, the dad recognized that he was being manipulated.

"I'm sorry you feel that way. But you are responsible for your actions. I can't take the blame for what you do because I don't have control over you. You will have to suffer the consequences of your bad choices. Neither one of us can change the past, but you can change the effect the past has on you now, son. Remember that I'll always love you, and I'm here for you. But I cannot and will not accept the blame for your decisions."

When we parents believe we are supposed to take the responsibility for our kids' behavior, we set ourselves up for many frustrations, untold disappointments, and a groundswell of guilt. We become easily manipulated and wind up becoming the proverbial co-dependent, enabling parent.

Kathryn learned this principle the hard way when another parent demanded that she apologize for the actions of her children.

All the youngsters involved were in their late teens. Kathryn's kids were sophisticated and had grown up in the United States. They had taken some naive missionary kids out one evening to a rock concert which hadn't been approved by either set of parents. In the midst of that rather free-spirited setting, the worldly kids taught their innocent friends how to smoke marijuana. What humiliation for Kathryn when the truth was told.

Of course she was sick at heart, and would have done anything in her power to prevent the incident. When confronted by the other parents, Kathryn swallowed hard, and explained how deeply she regretted what had happened. She promised to have a serious talk about it with her children. "But," she added, "I can't undo the damage that's been done. In fact, I can't even guarantee a formal apology."

"I don't see why not," the missionary mom snapped in disapproval.

Kathryn took a deep breath and went on. "Look, all of our kids are old enough to make some very poor choices on their own. And I don't think we parents can take the responsibility for every wrong thing they decide to do."

Beware of the Pharisees—They're Back!

Churches can be a great comfort to parents in pain. But, as we noted before, at times there are situations where well-intentioned Christians can add fuel to our fires of anguish. In Bible days there was a group of religious individuals called the Pharisees. They were judgmental, self-righteous people, and they are still stalking around in religious circles today. When the Pharisees saw Jesus talking with a blind man, they posed their question: "Master, who sinned so that this man was born blind? Was it his parents?" Can you imagine? They were operating on the theory that if something went wrong, someone had sinned. Jesus knew how mistaken they were and quickly put the issue to rest.

"No one has sinned," said Jesus, "but this happened so that the glory of God should be revealed in him." At that point He healed the blind man, much to the Pharisees' annoyance.

Those Pharisees would be among those who glibly say, "Well, good parents have good kids and a bad parent will end up with a bad kid." Today's Pharisees, like those of Jesus' time, are always more concerned with pointing out the faults of others than with loving people just the way they are.

Haven't we all known wonderful, caring parents with defiant, uncaring children? Sometimes a family will have two or three "perfect" kids and one "black sheep." And I know more than one set of absentee, and even abusive, parents who have the most loving kids imaginable.

Good Behavior Comes from Within

When our children are small, it is our responsibility to instill within them a good value system. As Christians, along with a sense of right and wrong, we also need to teach them to feel an awareness of God, and to inspire them to love Him. That way their moral decisions will be motivated by a God-consciousness, and hopefully with a personal relationship with Him.

A twelve-year-old boy sat down next to his mom one night and asked, "Mom, will you forgive me for cussing yesterday?"

She looked at her son in surprise. "I didn't hear you cuss yesterday. When did that happen? What did you say?"

"Oh, I was outside playing and Mark crashed into me. It really made me mad because he hurt my leg pretty bad. So before I knew it, I called him a @#%*!"

Suffice it to say that the word David had used to describe Mark was one of the most obscene words he could have possibly chosen. His mother stared at him in disbelief.

"That's an awful thing to call anybody! Why would you ever want to use that word? All he did was run into you by accident. Good grief, Dave."

"Yeah, I know. That's why I want you to forgive me."

At that moment, David's mom came to a sad-but-true realization.

"David," she sighed. "I can't forgive you, because you didn't do anything against me. You'll have to ask the Lord to forgive you."

"But you don't like me to cuss."

"I know, and I appreciate your telling me. But I can only be responsible for what you do in our house or in my hearing. If I *hear* you talk that way, you'll not only owe me an apology, I'll have to discipline you. That kind of language is completely inappropriate for anyone to use. But the things you do that I don't know about are between you and God. You'd better take it up with Him. I'll be glad to pray with you, if you want me to."

A Lesson in Accountability

At times, an inappropriate sense of guilt plagues us; it lurks in the shadows and accuses us, day and night. False guilt endeavors to convince us we're just not cut out for this parenting stuff. If we would only work less, try harder, or pray more, we could whip those kids into shape. Are we the ones who will give account of those kids before God?

If we have done all we can to bring up our boys and girls "in the nurture and admonition of the Lord" during their formative years, we simply have to let go of them later on. If we haven't done all we should have, there are some steps we can take to rectify that situation. (We will discuss them in a later chapter.) But whether we have done the best we could or not, the Bible advises:

> **EVERY ONE OF US SHALL GIVE**
> **ACCOUNT OF HIMSELF**
> **TO GOD (ROM. 14:12)**

Did God say, "Every one shall give account of his spouse, his children, his friends, his relatives, and anyone else who crosses his path"? How could He? How can we be responsible for anyone over whom we are not granted control? If I had a grip on my children's keys to happiness and behavior, things might have taken a different course from time to time. But we hold the keys only for ourselves.

You are only accountable for you! Isn't that a sweet relief? Here's a wonderful piece of writing that sums it all up so well.

IT'S YOUR MOVE, CHILD

I gave you life,
   but cannot live it for you.
I can teach you things,
   but I cannot make you learn
I can give you directions,
   but I cannot always be there to lead you.
I can allow you freedom,
   but I cannot account for it.
I can take you to church,
   but I cannot make you believe.
I can teach you right from wrong,
   but I can't always decide for you.
I can buy you beautiful clothes,
   but I cannot make you lovely inside.
I can offer you advice,
   but I cannot accept it for you.
I can give you love,
   but I cannot force it upon you.
I can teach you to be a friend,
   but I cannot make you one.
I can teach you to share,
   but I cannot make you unselfish.
I can teach you respect,
   but I cannot force you to show honor.
I can grieve about your report card,
   but I cannot doubt your teacher.
I can advise you about friends,
   but I cannot choose them for you.
I can teach you about sex,
   but I cannot keep you pure.
I can tell you the facts of life,
   but I cannot build your reputation.
I can tell you about drinking,
   but I cannot say NO for you.
I can warn you about drugs,
   but I cannot prevent you from using them.

I can tell you about lofty goals,
>   but I cannot achieve them for you.
I can teach you kindness,
>   but I cannot force you to be gracious.
I can warn you about sin,
>   but I cannot make you moral.
I can pray for you,
>   but I cannot make you walk with God.
I can teach you about Jesus,
>   but I cannot make Him your Savior.
I can tell you how to live,
>   but I cannot give you eternal life.

Source Unknown

5

Blame Removal Therapy

Relief from Guilt Pangs

In the early years of psychological enlightenment, we parents were the scapegoats for everything: bedwetting, smoking, alcoholism—you name the fault, and the folks were to blame. It was all the parents' fault. We were naughty parents if we had naughty kids.

Let's explore this crippling question of who is to blame for the condition of our kids. This question paralyzes us because we are terribly afraid that parents are the ones to blame. We can see the disapproving judge's gavel pounding down with the verdict, "Parents Guilty."

What Makes Us the Way We Are?

The age-old question, "Why is my kid the way he is?" has been pondered for centuries by parents in pain. Is it a question of heredity or environment? Personality or parenting? The answer is that it is all of the above; it is not an either/or situation. Children are a product of many contributing factors, including:

Heredity

Parental input

Genetics

Other adults

Nationality traits

Persuasion of friends

Environmental agents

Influence of past experiences

Personality

Temperament

Talents

Gifts

Strengths

Weaknesses

Human behavior cannot be traced to one single source. Like most issues in life, it is a very complex one. We wouldn't want to assume that a person has died of cancer solely because he or she had bad eating habits. A heart attack doesn't occur simply because someone didn't exercise. We've all heard about some health-conscious person who develops cancer despite good oat bran consumption or another who had a heart attack while jogging. In the same sense, unhealthy behavior cannot be linked to any one contributing factor.

Dr. Dobson writes in *Parenting Isn't for Cowards,*

This tendency to assume the responsibility for everything our teenagers and grown children do is not only a product of psychological mumbo-jumbo (determinism), but it reflects our own vulnerabilities as parents. We know we are flawed. We know how often we fail. Even under the best of circumstances, we are forced time after time to guess at what is right for our children. Errors in judgment occur. Then our own selfishness surfaces and we do and say things that can never be undone. All these shortcomings are then magnified tenfold when a son or daughter goes bad.

Stop the Parent Bashing!

I loved the title of the book on the shelf: *What My Parents Did Right.* Author Gloria Gaither wrote it as an antidote to the kind of parent bashing that goes on all around us. She writes,

> . . . my love for God came early in life. Through their day-to-day activities and with their very being, my mother and father taught me about God and about serving Him. That's just one of the many things my parents did right.

Some parents are more good than bad; others are more bad than good. Sometimes we have to be careful not to throw the baby out with the bath water when we're looking at our past. Even bad parents can give good "gifts" to their children.

A woman named Claire came up to me after a seminar. We got to talking about her background, and she made an interesting observation. "You know, before I became a Christian, I was into alcohol, marijuana, and promiscuous sex. When my father drank too much he sexually abused us kids. And even though my mom knew about it, she did nothing to stop him. I've come a long way, baby." She laughed infectiously.

Even when you've heard that kind of story a thousand times, it's always shocking. I looked at Claire compassionately. "Has it been hard for you to forgive your parents?"

She nodded with a smile. "For the first few years of my Christian walk, I shut them out of my mind completely and focused my attention on getting my own act together, changing my habits and leaving the past behind. But eventually I had to deal with my parents and my relationship with them. But that's what I wanted to tell you about—in the process of forgiving my parents for their failures, I've discovered something interesting."

"What's that?" I asked.

"I've come to appreciate some very good qualities that they instilled in me, even in the midst of all the craziness. You see, they weren't all bad. They both had a great sense of humor, and they taught me to laugh at my troubles. And when my dad wasn't drinking, he was more fun than anyone. He'd take all us kids for outings, and everybody loved him."

"But isn't it kind of hard to overlook all the bad things that happened?"

Claire thoughtfully continued. "You know, we're all good and bad. In every relationship, we have to overlook something we don't like. In the case of my parents, what went on was extremely emotionally destructive. But once I was really able to forgive them, I actually began to love them and to value them for the good things they taught me. I know better than to trust them in certain areas, but I guess I've decided just to leave the ugly stuff with God."

Not everyone is able to reach the kind of peace Claire found with her dysfunctional family. Some parents are too intolerable for healthy relationships ever to take root between them and their kids. But one thing bears repeating: we cannot allow our parents' unwise input to overshadow the way we conduct our own parenting responsibilities today; it will surely influence us, but does not have to control us. With God's help, we are capable of changing the negative effects of the past and the way they impact our present way of life.

What's Done Is Done

In a similar sense, parents can't allow their children's pasts to overwhelm them as they treat them in the present. This is especially true for those who have adopted a child. Adoptive parents may attribute rebellious behavior to unknown factors that transpired during formative months or years. The questions that arise may never be answered. "Was he abused? Rejected? Emotionally damaged before we even got him?" Chances are the truth will never be known.

As a stepparent who raised two children who are not my birthchildren, allow me to remind you again of a vital principle: God chose for you to have *this* child. *These* children. In that case, He must be planning on you giving them your very best. The rest is up to Him.

Sometimes it's hard to pin down the contributing factors that led to our own behavior. I'd have to describe myself in pop-psych terms as "raised in a dysfunctional family," "verbally abused," "physically abused," "a victim," and who knows what else! Like Claire, although these terms might *explain* my behavior, I've learned that they certainly don't *excuse* it. I cannot blame my mother for my cellulite just because she was the one who taught me to swallow my troubles and chase them down with a milkshake.

And, yes, my earthly dad was a poor father role model. But his inadequacy does not have to cripple me in relating to God my Father. I believe my parents were responsible for what they did then; I am responsible for what I do now.

> ## VIEW YOUR BIRTHPARENTS SIMPLY AS THE BIOLOGICAL INSTRUMENTS OF YOUR EXISTENCE

My parents tried to do their part, and parented to the best of their ability, impaired and disabled as they may have been. My parents were fully accountable for what they did in my growing up days, but I am responsible for who I am today, because I "hold the key."

How much are my own parents to blame for the way I am today? Not at all. How much credit can they take for me today? None.

> ## PARENTS CANNOT CLAIM THE CREDIT OR THE BLAME

Coping with Devastating News

If you are struggling with an undue sense of responsibility about your children's choices, perhaps it's because you are trying to deal with some extremely difficult circumstances. What is it that has broken your heart?

More and more parents today are facing one of the most devastating announcements any child can make—that he (or she) is pursuing a gay lifestyle. In recent years, the closet door has been flung open, and when parents find their own kids inside, it is almost always a painful blow. This particular circumstance tends to be even more deeply crushing to Christian parents. And while those in the gay community would like to explain their preferences as the results of some "past life" experience, or from having been "born this way," there are no statistics available to verify any such theories.

Although some past abusive experience may predispose a child to homosexuality, like any other antisocial behavior we've discussed, the child must make a conscious choice to adopt an alternative lifestyle.

And how should you accept such news? Barbara Johnson, who faced this concern with her son Larry, has written several books about coping with life's cruelest struggles. In *Stick a Geranium in Your Hat and Be Happy,* she describes her own response.

> In my desperate attempts to make him respond, I had uttered threats and unloving things like, "I would rather have you be DEAD than be a homosexual!" At that moment I loved Larry, but I hated that part of him. I wanted to hug him, but I wanted to kill him—I was a kaleidoscope of emotional shock. It would be later that I learned that parents say all kinds of unreal thing to their kids when they learn they are homosexual. In my own emotional frenzy, all I could do was quote Bible verses about homosexuality. And all the while I was also denying that this could really be happening to us.

A few pages later, Barbara quotes a poem which has comforted many parents.

> Acceptance is the answer to all my problems today.
> When I am disturbed, it is because I find some
>   person, place, thing or situation—
> Some fact of my life—unacceptable to me, and I can
>   find no serenity until I accept that person,
>   place, thing or situation as being exactly the
>   way it is supposed to be at this moment.
> Nothing, absolutely nothing happens in God's world
>   by mistake.
> Unless I accept life completely on life's terms, I
>   cannot be happy.

I need to concentrate not so much on what needs to
    be changed in the world
As on what needs to be changed in me and my
    attitudes.

Source Unknown

The Buck Stops . . . Where?

Have you ever played the Blame Game? I'm tired of
it! Our parents were peddling as fast as they could; they
were doing all they were capable of doing at the time. No
parents should be held responsible now for what they
didn't know "back then." Not them. Not us.

Every parent alive has made mistakes along the
way. Some of those poor decisions may have been small.
Others may have been disastrous and irreversible. Will
our children have to suffer for our sinful behavior? These
verses from Ezekiel 18 help us answer that strategic
question:

> The word of the LORD came to me: "What do you
> people mean by quoting this proverb about the land
> of Israel:
>
> " 'The fathers eat sour grapes,
>   and the children's teeth are set on edge'?"
>
> "As surely as I live, declares the Sovereign LORD,
> you will no longer quote this proverb in Israel. For
> every living soul belongs to me, the father as well as
> the son—both alike belong to me. The soul who sins
> is the one who will die."
>
> Ezekiel 18:1–4 NIV

In verse 20, God concludes: "*The son will not share
the guilt of the father, nor will the father share the guilt of
the son.* The righteousness of the righteous man will be

credited to him, and the wickedness of the wicked will be charged against him" (emphasis mine).

God's word leaves little doubt about parental responsibility. Yet we know there are certain things for which we are very much responsible. What are they? Having established that we honestly don't hold anyone else's key to happiness, we may find our pockets empty. However, we are not scot-free.

Parental accountability can be summed up in a nutshell: before God we have a responsibility TO, not FOR our children. Before God, parents are responsible TO their child:

TO train him up, in the way he should go

TO be an example

TO be sincere, honest, open

TO accept that child, unconditionally

TO love, as best we can

TO ask forgiveness when we have failed

TO pray

If we'll be honest, we'll say we have our hands full! Our charge is to be fully accountable for our own actions. It will take all our parental emotional energy to fulfill this responsibility, before God, TO our children.

At the same time, we are beginning to realize we are *not* responsible:

FOR his attitudes

FOR his choices

FOR his friends

FOR his lack of interest in church

FOR his anger and resentment

The picture is clear. We cannot affect change inside our kids (or anyone else either!) because we do not have access to the thoughts and intents of their hearts.

> KIDS ARE RESPONSIBLE FOR
> THEIR ACTIONS.
> PARENTS ARE RESPONSIBLE FOR
> THEIR REACTIONS.

Of course, if we find that our children are developing bad attitudes, nasty habits, or other disturbing behaviors, we owe it to them to ask ourselves why and investigate the trail. We need to know if we've blown it. Or not "been there" at some important juncture. We need to know these things in order to make amends and rebuild relationships. Constant attention to maintaining open channels in relationships is of vital importance, both for our children's health and for our own sanity.

Quick to Listen, Slow to Speak

My single parent friend Annie and I were discussing these life-saving principles about the same time her fourteen-year-old son informed her, "Mom, I'm gonna pierce my ear!"

Annie's first inclination was to gasp, "What? No way will I let you do that." Just then the realization hit her that her son was not requesting her permission. He was simply informing her of his intentions.

Calculating with lightning speed (as only a mom can do), she drew a deep breath and calmly stated her case. "I have a bit of a problem with that." Swallowing hard, she continued, "Which ear, honey?"

Her heart was pounding by now. We live in California—we know the implications of such a question, since some gay men identify themselves with a ring in the right ear.

"I want a fake diamond on my left ear."

(Whew! Passed that one.)

About now Annie began to inventory the many things she'd said no to before. Her son had often disobeyed anyway. She chose her words carefully, sheepishly offering her unsolicited advice.

"Well, my concern is that you'll soon be looking for a job, and an earring may not look so good to a serious employer. And then there are the friends it might attract to you; I think it signals something harsh about you that isn't really you. I would love you anyway, but once you make that decision, you'll always have that mark. I don't think it's a smart idea."

Annie could barely look at him for fear her eyes would give away her real feelings. She desperately wanted to stop him in his tracks and scream, "No! Absolutely not!" Her son casually strolled off, as Annie sank into a heap, a silent prayer on her lips.

For days afterward, every time her son came through the door, Annie would check out his ears with a quick glance. For some unknown reason he never carried through with his intention. Was it because Mom didn't overreact? Was it because he took her advice to heart? Who knows? Meanwhile, Mom had passed the "responsible TO not FOR" test with flying colors.

Avoiding the Guilt Trap

This same principle holds water in all our personal relationships. We're fully responsible:

TO be faithful to our spouse . . . not FOR the choices our spouse may make.

TO make emotionally healthy choices . . . not FOR the emotional health of another.

TO our friends to be caring . . . not FOR the purpose of being their emotional pit stop.

TO our place of work . . . not FOR the outcome of the organization.

TO be honoring to our own parents . . . not FOR their unhappiness.

Dealing with my own mother is the first arena in which I learned this principle. Unfortunately for me, Mother is the West Coast distributor for guilt. (She has a franchise.) My mother is an active travel agent for guilt trips.

Because she felt I had her "key to happiness" and she was miserable, I wasn't doing my job as a daughter. She'd complain, "I gave you the best years of my life. You never write. You never call . . . I know you are busy helping other people, but you could bring a little happiness to your own mother once in awhile. I know you're not coming home for Christmas again—that's OK; I just won't put up the tree . . . ."

Pow! When we think we are responsible FOR someone else, the condemnation comes pounding against us. But now I simply examine myself; have I been doing my job in obligation TO her as an adult daughter? Is she in proper place in my life's priorities? Once I've worked through these considerations, I am able to properly ward off the slings and arrows of outrageous guilt trips.

A parent can not only survive, but can thrive! Let's all swallow the truth of this pain-killing prescription:

> **GAIN A CLEAR UNDERSTANDING OF WHO IS ACTUALLY RESPONSIBLE FOR WHAT.**

With every year that your child grows and develops, your potential for blame diminishes. Little children count on their parents for all sorts of guidance, instruction, and inspiration. But the older the child, the less the influence. And once your son or daughter is old enough to make his own adult decisions, the true Judge, who judges each person according to his own deeds, divides up the responsibility fairly.

Does your child have a bad attitude toward church? Parents, repeat aloud, "I am not responsible for his bad attitudes."

Did you raise a child who is defiant and unruly? Then repeat after me, "I am not responsible for his bad choices."

Does your child hate school or lie about attendance? Then repeat after me, "I am not responsible for his behavior."

Does your child have destructive habits or compulsions?

Does your child refuse to conduct himself morally and responsibly?

Does your child partake in a lifestyle that is inappropriate to your value system?

Let the courtroom recess and the judge retire to his chambers. Parents have already been pronounced "Not Guilty."

We're often reminded in self-help books and psychological seminars that guilt isn't a valid emotion for Christians. This teaching is based on the fact that our sins have been paid for by the Son of God, who came from heaven to take our legal penalties as His own on the cross. Yet we often find ourselves struggling in a protracted battle with regret and shame, going over the same guilty ground again and again.

Perhaps we feel it's necessary to demonstrate repeatedly our repentance to God. Or maybe we feel that our misery is a kind of "dues paying" for the past. In either case, true faith requires us to release the shame and the blame to the One who paid the price, the One who has removed all our shortcomings as far as the east from the west. When we refuse to receive Jesus' forgiveness and peace, we are really playing God, choosing to condemn ourselves and emotionally overruling His work of redemption.

This is not to say that we won't feel a twinge of pain over a prodigal son or daughter. Of course there is pain. There is a sense of loss. There is a longing for change. But these things do not have the same crippling quality as guilt. And it's my prayer that, by now, we are also sensing the hope that no matter what our parental failures have been, we can entrust what's been left undone to our heavenly Father.

As His Word so beautifully promises,

> And we know that in all things God works for the good of those who love him, who have been called according to his purpose.
>
> Romans 8:28 NIV

In the meantime, consider some wisdom from a mother who has suffered through her own times of prayer and pain over her children. In *Prodigals and Those Who Love Them,* Ruth Bell Graham writes,

> A FEW SUGGESTIONS FOR ME AS A MOTHER
> Keep communications open at all times.
> Permit person-to-person collect phone calls.
> Let them know they are loved and welcome at
>   home.
> Permit the children to disagree with me,
>   provided they do it respectfully. (And I

find occasionally they are right and I am
wrong.)
Make a clear distinction between moral and
nonmoral issues.
Encourage.

6

The Prodigal Syndrome

Anticipating a Childhood Disease

I SAT NEXT TO A MAN ON A PLANE who made the most astonishing statement.

"Well, it won't happen to *my* kids," he grinned, his arms folded smugly across his chest. "My kids won't rebel because my wife and I have done everything by the book. We've researched child development, gone to communications seminars, and involved them in all sorts of sports and academic activities."

I could hardly believe what I was hearing. I asked, "So what makes you think they won't rebel anyway?"

"Look, dear, there's no way they're going to rebel," he said patronizingly. "My kids respect me and my wife too much. We're all the best of friends."

"How old are your kids?"

"The boys are in fifth and sixth grade, and our daughter is five—she'll start kindergarten in September."

I nodded, and buried my nose in a magazine while I thought about this man's confident, almost arrogant words. I certainly hoped he was right—it was obvious that he would be shattered by anything less than compliant, cooperative kids. But his beliefs sounded vaguely familiar. Hadn't I heard others express the same point of view, usually cloaked in Christian platitudes? Hadn't I once dreamed about such pie-in-the-sky visions myself?

Facing the Possibilities

One morning a neighbor woman telephoned. She was terribly upset because she had to inform me that her teenage son had borrowed her car and promptly crashed it into mine, which was parked in the street.

"I'll pay for all the damages . . . I'm so sorry. Tell me, do you have children?"

"Yes I do—I have two girls in elementary school."

Later, when I received her check in the mail, I noticed she had written it for more than enough to cover the damages. I called to tell her about the overpayment.

"Never mind," she sighed. "Just buy something for your girls while you still LIKE them."

I guess you could say the "prodigal syndrome" is a late-childhood disease that's been going around for centuries. And, sad to say, there's no vaccination against it.

The fact is, I don't know any parents of older kids who haven't worked through periods of difficulty with their children. The degrees of conflict vary, of course, but the challenge usually becomes very real and very frightening.

Let's be kind to ourselves by developing realistic expectations. If we don't face the possibilities of what can happen, we're setting ourselves up for major disappointments when and if they do. If I'm driving to the airport, I expect the traffic flow to move along at a certain speed. But what if the traffic slows down due to an accident, and backs up? If I didn't allow for that, I'll find myself feeling nervous, fighting anxiety, and maybe even missing my flight.

| HOPE FOR THE BEST |
| PREPARE FOR THE WORST |

Those eight words might sum up the proper posture. If we as parents factor in "The Prodigal Syndrome" as a possible obstacle to be faced in our child's future, we will be better able to cope should the time arrive. And, assuming it does, it may come in the guise of a strange-looking hairdo that lasts about a week, or it could be around for eleven years and leave many scars. In any case, it is a transition, or passage, toward maturity through which our children must somehow pass.

One way or another, children begin to grow away from their parents. They try their wings. And, ultimately, they fly.

The Prodigal Parable

Just about everyone is familiar with the New Testament parable of the Prodigal Son. If you haven't read it, you may want to—it's found in the book of Luke, in chapter 15, verses 11 through 32.

We can't be sure that the prodigal's wise father had braced himself for the inevitable, but he certainly exhibited poise and patience when the worst case scenario occurred. He had the presence of mind to conduct himself with dignity when his son's rebellion struck the family. The younger son confronted the dad: "I want my share of your estate now, instead of waiting until you die!" His father agreed to divide his wealth between his sons (Luke 15:12 TLB).

Here was a hurting father who desperately wanted this financial confrontation to come to an end. He never argued, but graciously dealt out what was due the son. He must have known that the boy would abuse his new-found freedom, and was not mature enough to handle money. But Dad didn't take one last shot as his boy headed down the driveway, either—"You brat, you'll blow it all! Don't say I didn't warn you!"

If this dad had been aware of the "happiness key" concept, I'm sure he would have been tempted to grasp his son's key and whack him with it! But Dad was endeavoring to practice being responsible TO, not FOR his son. The handwriting was on the wall, so the father gave to the son what was asked for, not in a sense of surrender or abandonment, but in faith.

Here was a dad willing to allow his son to reap the inevitable consequences of his bad attitudes. He didn't want to object, and postpone or delay the swift completion of the cycle. Of course, he must have felt that the sooner it came to an end, the better, but he let it run its course. I'm sure the dad must have whispered under his breath the words of comfort which King David penned in Psalm 139, "If I make my bed in hell, behold, thou art there." He was trusting God to apprehend the son sometime, somewhere, somehow, in the midst of his prodigal experience.

Our friend Frank has always struggled with Frank, Jr. in their father-son relationship; the two are total opposites. Despite their differences, Frank, who is president of a family-owned building development business, has done his best to maintain a positive attitude and to believe the best about Frank, Jr. Unfortunately, no matter how much "believing" Frank, Sr., did, nothing seemed to motivate his son.

The boy had somehow completed college, but without ever giving any explanation, he refused to dive into a career. Junior was lazy and shiftless—content to do nothing. How could he have come from a family of such highly-motivated movers and shakers?

Dad kept hinting around about the work ethic, about the family history of hard-working providers, about the unlikeliness of winning the lottery, and about the satsifaction and benefits of making money. But nothing moved the son out of bed in the morning—except tennis dates with long-legged ladies. After years of enabling the boy to stay unemployed by providing room and board at no cost, Dad finally kicked him out of the house. Of course he hoped that this move would compel Junior to get a job.

No such luck.

Within a month's time, the son showed up married— to an older woman who was more than wealthy enough to support him. Not too many years later, she grew weary of her toy-boy, and ended the marriage. After the divorce (which had been a given from day one), Frank, Jr., "came to himself," as was said of the prodigal son.

As he related his experiences, he explained that his only regret was that dear old Dad hadn't kicked him out sooner!

Meanwhile, back in the New Testament . . .

Who knows how long the prodigal's father stood gazing down the road, yearning to see the return of his son. The Bible confirms the son blew the money "on riotous living"; Dad must have pictured the son homeless and penniless by now.

But no matter. His door was open for the son's return; he had apparently made that clear. The son didn't expect to hear "I told you so . . . you should have listened." The boy knew he'd be welcomed when he came back. Truly, love "bears all things."

Without excusing, enabling, or abandoning his own standards and principles, the father waited, in faith. He hoped, as Dr. Robert Schuller puts it, that "God will *use* what He does not *choose*." He prayed that God would somehow "make all things work together for good" for his returning prodigal.

When the son came back, very much the worse for the wear, he was clearly a wiser man. He claimed he was not "worthy" to work in the family business, but he revealed a willing heart to stick around as a servant. Dad began the celebration in spite of the objection of the prodigal's older brother, who disapproved of the festivities. "My brother doesn't deserve it," he objected, jealous and frustrated.

What parent only gives what a child deserves? Do we feed them because they deserve it? Do they get clothes only because they have earned them? Are they sent to school because they've warranted this privilege? No, a parent gives because he loves.

I imagine the younger son returned home in pretty bad shape. After living with swine for awhile, you're bound to start smelling like one. I'm sure it was not pleasant for the prodigal's parents to see the deterioration of their "baby," knowing that he would forever bear the scars of his little adventure.

Staying Ahead of the Game

Are you concerned about your own child? Do you have a sneaking suspicion that he or she is involved in unhealthy or even illegal activities? Perhaps the uncertainty is driving you crazy. Most of us know that . . .

> THE TRUTH WILL SET US FREE,
> BUT FIRST IT WILL PROBABLY
> MAKE US MISERABLE.

In the meantime, should we search the room? Should we wait up to see what time they really come home? Do we dare get a closer look at this latest boyfriend? (At least all his tattoos are spelled correctly.) Is ignorance bliss?

Denial seems delightful for awhile. I wear a T-shirt with a cartoon of Cleopatra's head on it. The caption reads, "The Queen of De Nile." I used to chicken out as a mom. I told myself, "I won't ask, because I don't want to hear it. I don't want to volunteer for another emotional eruption."

Our confidence wobbles when we begin to sense an erosion of trust. We notice certain disturbing traits developing . . .

Attitude changes

More time spent isolated in the bedroom

Questionable friends

Curfew violations

Avoiding communication

Deteriorating physical appearance and/or health

I know how you feel. You tell yourself that each symptom is "no biggie . . . not to worry," but it continues to gnaw at you. You don't want to become an accusing, suspicious parent, snooping around their bedrooms. But you find yourself frustrated and blurting out,

"I know what you're doing!"

"You smell like smoke . . ."

"You can't fool me any more!"

And when accused, the same emotional backlash comes, "You don't trust me!" But a track record of lies does not make a firm foundation for trust. If this describes your plight, congratulations! You have just entered a new stage of parenting. You are beginning to . . .

> ## LOOK FOR A WAY OF
> ## LOVING WITHOUT TRUSTING

At this point, it's a healthy exercise for parents to face their own feelings and disappointments and bring them into the light. This can be done in the letter-writing exercise, "A Very Special Love Letter," at the end of this chapter. Why not come out of denial, not only about your child's activities, but about your own feelings. Whether or not your child ever sees this letter from you, you will have been able to face and process the pain you are experiencing.

> ## PARENTS: BE PREPARED FOR
> ## THE PRODIGAL SYNDROME!

Drs. David and Jan Stoop, who work together as Christian psychologists, struggled and experienced deep pain due to their prodigal son who spent many years as a drug addict. "It was progressive," remarks Jan. "First I was the mother of the trouble-maker; then mother of the jailbird. Then the druggie. Then the homeless."

Today their ex–heroin-addict son is serving God on the mission field. "Keep the big picture in mind," says Dave. "Hang on. Believe God will intervene. You never know when the miracle will come!"

Paying Their Dues

Dr. Stoop's good words are encouraging. But there are times when it seems as if our lives are consumed by the bad decisions of our children, no matter how old our kids are.

One mother bitterly snapped at me, "It's not fair. My whole life has to be altered. I have to learn about drug

addiction because my kid is a drug addict. I have to suffer with the unpleasantness of an ex-son-in-law because my daughter wanted a divorce. They make lousy choices, and we parents have to survive the consequences. It's not fair," she repeated, her face stained with tears.

And she's absolutely right. It isn't fair. If life were fair, people would be granted permission to fly up over the pigeons once in a while to even up the score. But that'll never happen. We wind up being in the "bad things happen to good people" category.

Must our kids pay for their shortcomings?

Does God make them pay for our mistakes?

Must they suffer all their lives for their prodigal phase?

The good news of the Gospel shouts NO! to all questions of retribution. Jesus died to cancel all our debts. No one else can make compensation for them, for us, for anyone. However, there are natural consequences that result from prodigal adventures, and they are unavoidable.

Angela's twenty-year-old son turned his back on his Christian upbringing. Before long, he developed an addiction to both alcohol and cigarettes. Meanwhile, he was building up a formidable number of debts, including unpaid traffic tickets, credit card balances, and personal loans. He soon owed almost $20,000.

Finally, Angela's prodigal came full circle—as the Bible says, his belly was "full of it." But when he returned to his folks and to the Lord, his debts and habits did not magically disappear. Mom and Dad had their son back home, but not exactly in the best condition. The conversion of this prodigal did not magically clear up his lungs or immediately change his habits. He will still have to "pay the piper" to heal the emotional and physical scars he incurred.

And, as her son suffers, Angela suffers too. Even though she's let go. Even though she's responsible for her own happiness. Even though her prodigal has returned.

How are you really feeling about your problem child? I love the poem Ruth Bell Graham wrote when one of her sons was wandering away from the family.

> She waited for the call
> that never came;
> searched every mail for a letter,
> or a note,
> or card
> that bore his name;
> and on her knees
> at night,
> and on her feet
> all day,
> she stormed Heaven's gate
> in his behalf;
> she pled for him
> in Heaven's high court.
> "Be still, and wait, and see"—
> the word God gave;
> then she
> knew that He would
> do in and for and with him,
> that which she never could.
> So doubts ignored
> she went about her chores
> with you—
> knowing though spurned
> His word was true.
> The prodigal had not returned,
> but God was God,
> and there was work to do.
>
> Ruth Bell Graham

It may be that, as yet, you don't have a prodigal child. I pray that it will always be so. It may be that, although you and your child have had difficult times, she (or he) is still at home. Or you may be, like Mrs. Graham was, watching the mail, listening for the phone, watching for the car outside—longing for a lost child to return.

A Very Special Love Letter

Perhaps you have some things you'd like to say to your child, but cannot. Facing your emotions is good medicine, no matter what your feelings may be. One of my prescriptions for parents of prodigals (and others) is to write a letter to your child, a letter that you never intend to mail. In doing so you'll find it possible to identify your emotions, and you'll be better equipped to deal with them.

Such a letter should contain three important elements:

1. What the child has done
2. How you feel about it
3. What you want now

Here are some ideas for letters.

A Letter from Mom

Dear ___ ,
I need this opportunity to express myself to you. I need to get a few things off my chest. Because our relationship has so deteriorated, I've been avoiding facing my feelings, and want to do so now.

(Include next a discussion of what was done.)

So much water has gone over the bridge between

us; it almost seems as if the bridge is washed out. You began to show signs of mutiny at age __ when you . . .

At age __ you . . .

The things that have so disturbed me include *(be specific, but here are a few possibilities)* your behavior . . . your attitudes . . . your rejection of the church . . . your contempt for authority . . . bad habits . . . morals . . . choice of friends . . . the abortion . . .

(Discuss how you feel.)

I feel *(find the words that best apply)* scared . . . humiliated . . . confused . . . angry . . . frustrated . . . guilty . . .

(Perhaps some of the following thoughts may fit your circumstances . . . just think about your own reactions and try to put them into words, such as . . .)

I've sometimes wondered when and why you stopped loving me.

I remember praying for you before you were born, and having such great hopes and dreams for you.

I remember trying to answer your innocent questions about friends, politics, sports, and homework; I thought we had a good relationship.

Sometimes I can tell when you're lying, sometimes I can't.

Even though you've pulled the wool over my eyes so often, I still want to believe in you again.

I've blamed myself for everything. Then I blamed *(be specific)* the school . . . your friends . . . the divorce . . . the move . . .

(Next, discuss what you want now.)

First of all, I want you to forgive me for my part in our difficulties. I love you, and our relationship is more important to me than the issues that have come between us.

Won't you ask me to forgive you, too?

I want you to know that I don't have control over you, nor do I have any responsibility for you.

If you are angry with me still, I want to know how we can patch that up. In spite of all we've been through, I believe God loves each one of us, and can still fulfill His plan in our lives.

I'd like to listen to you so I can learn, not so I can change you. I pledge you my love; I'll always be here for you. I want to be able to embrace you again, without the uneasiness between us. I long for a free flow of caring exchanges.

Most of all, please understand, that in spite of the many mistakes I may have made, I really have tried to do my best. I want you to forgive me, and I want to forgive you.

Let's leave the rest to God.

With love,

Mom

A Letter from Dad

Sometimes fathers have different things to say to their children than mothers do. Some fathers feel guilty and responsible for their lack of involvement in their children's lives, feeling it may have contributed to a prodigal episode. If you're a hurting father, take a look at the following ideas.

Dear ___,

I've been thinking about our relationship and want you to know how important it is to me. I can't wholeheartedly go into the future without making sure I've cleared up the past.

Considering all the problems we're experiencing now, I've got to ask myself, as your dad, "Have I contributed to whatever is going on in your heart and mind?" If so, I really do want to know about it. Will you write out for me the things you may be holding against me?

I'd like a chance to talk to you about all this. I know I've failed you in some ways, and I can think of a number of them right now. Will you forgive me for . . .

I wish I'd been around more when you were growing up. I missed out on so much. I'm sorry I wasn't there for you for important games . . . recitals . . . open-house at school . . . *(fill in the things you remember)*. Somehow I was too busy, and it wasn't right.

By and large, I tried to do my best, and I want you to know that. I never meant to hurt you, and I guess I thought supporting you financially was more important than actually being with you. Looking back, I can see that wasn't quite right.

More than anything else, I'd like to establish a friendship with you from here on out. If you'd like the same, let's find a way to do it.

I love you, no matter what.

Dad

Perhaps our last word about prodigals here should be the words of Jesus—the prayer He prayed for all of us who know and love Him. His desire for us is always the same, whether we are walking closely beside Him or acting like prodigals ourselves. Let's thank Him for His

beautiful intercession for us, and then speak it out loud
to Him as our prayer for our own children.

> Holy Father, keep them in your own care—all
> those you have given me—so that they will be united
> just as we are, with none missing. . . . I'm not ask-
> ing you to take them out of the world, but to keep
> them safe from Satan's power. . . . Make them pure
> and holy through teaching them your words of truth.
> As you sent me into the world, I am sending them
> into the world, and I consecrate myself to meet their
> need for growth in truth and holiness. . . . Father, I
> want them with me.
>
> John 17:11–24 TLB

7

Cured Through Consequences

Time-Released Sowing and Reaping

IN THE GARDEN OF EDEN, EVERYTHING was beautiful, lovely, and tranquil. All was in order—except for God's children, Adam and Eve. After the snake-in-the-grass convinced them that an apple a day would be good for their health, God dismissed them from the Garden. This was the first historical example of "sowing and reaping." As Josh McDowell and Dick Day wrote in their book *How to Be a Hero to Your Kids:*

> Tempted by the serpent, Eve ate from the tree, and then Adam followed suit. When God discovered what had happened, the consequences came swiftly. Adam and Eve became susceptible to physical death, and all its related penalties, such as pain in childbirth, living by the sweat of one's brow and banishment from Paradise itself (see Genesis 3:1–19).
>
> God had spelled out the boundaries in which Adam and Eve could operate, and when they chose to violate or to cross those boundaries, they had to face the consequences. Yet God did not set these limits until He had first demonstrated His love by

providing for their every need—physically, emotionally, rationally, socially, sexually, and spiritually. When He set limits, God was giving Adam and Even an opportunity to respond to His love by trusting and obeying.

Parenting children works much the same way. Parents are responsible to spell out the boundaries for their children. These are the limits that you build upon the loving foundation you have already established. By laying down limits, you make the child accountable for his actions and behavior.

God held the first man and woman accountable, all right. They were told to pack up their fig leaves and hit the road. The Lord gave them some instructions which they were to carry out "east of Eden." "Be fruitful and multiply," he told them, and this time they obeyed. I've often wondered if that commandment was a blessing or part of the curse!

They were fruitful, to be sure. They had two fruits, Cain and Abel, who coauthored the first book on sibling rivalry. And so began the difficult parenting cycle. God's children, Adam and Eve, experienced what the principle of sowing and reaping means, long before the Apostle Paul penned it in Galatians 6:7.

> Be not deceived; God is not mocked; for whatsoever a man soweth, that shall he also reap.

The Rescuers (Not a Disney Cartoon)

God has always tried to warn His children that we will harvest what we plant. If we plant corn, we reap corn. If we plant trouble, we reap trouble. And if our kids plant problems, they should not reap rescue efforts from Mom and Dad!

Just as our attempts to "make the kids happy" begin at the cradle, the rescue pattern begins early, too.

The baby stubbornly demands attention by screaming, sounding like a mating call for a car alarm. Mom smiles tenderly, "Bless his precious little heart. He must be hungry again."

The toddler throws a temper tantrum, and the dad excuses it with, "Well, that poor little angel. She didn't have her nap today."

The preschooler keeps interrupting while we're trying to talk to someone. We reward him with a mouthful of Gummi Bears, guaranteed to glue his teeth together and thus keep him quiet.

The school-age child forgets to do his quarterly book report. "My sweet baby, you didn't mean to play Super Mario Brothers for nine straight hours, now did you? Of course you can stay home from school—your eyes look awfully tired, honey."

And then what happens? Our older kids come home and say:

- "I've lost my job, Mom—my boss never did like me. How can I make my car payments?"

- "I got arrested for driving under the influence. I can't afford the fine—it's $3,000. And besides, I'd only had one beer. That cop totally ripped me off when he gave me the breathalyzer test."

- "Looks like I'll be moving back home; Jim and I broke up last night. He's such a jerk—if I'd known what he was like, I'd have never asked him to leave his wife in the first place."

- "Yo, Dad? Yeah, like they found cocaine in my glove compartment, man. Yeah, but it

wasn't mine, Dad. Like, bummer, man. I don't
know how it got there!"

- "Mom, I'm pregnant—I guess Joe's vasectomy
was a big lie. Anyway, the abortion is scheduled for tomorrow morning. Could you drive
me?"

My late father-in-law, the beloved Dr. Herbert Ezell,
would always chuckle as he told the story of an irresponsible collegiate, who sent this SOS note home. It read,

DEAR DAD:
NO MON . . . NO FUN,
YOUR SON

Dad quickly replied,

DEAR SON:
TOO BAD . . . SO SAD,
YOUR DAD

How many excuses are there in the world? More than
can be counted. And what shall I do when I'm confronted
with a brand new array of excuses? Should I ask more questions? Should I continue to believe the best? Should I agree
with my child to protect our relationship? Should I subsi-
dize my son until he gets a break? Shall we send her back
for more classes at the University of Endless Education?

There is still something in most of us that continually
says, "Aw, why not? Give 'em another chance." But do our
well-intentioned efforts genuinely assist with our youngsters' development? Do we imagine our sons and daughters will feel indebted to us because of our unfailing
benevolence? The truth is that once we have been duped,
our kids will not respect us for it. Their appreciation will

not last. And our blind assistance will not lead them to repentance.

You know the parental phrase "this hurts me worse than it hurts you"? That's supposed to be about paddling little bottoms or sending grumpy ten-year-olds to sit in corners. We're not supposed to hurt worse than they do when they are grown up. Our pain is not supposed to last forever! After the child's age of accountability (and the procurement of his own "key"), our son or daughter should be the one experiencing the consequences of choices—not us!

Somehow we've got to stop paying the price for our "of age" kids. No wonder they're out with their friends while we're struggling to undo their damage. We must come to the place of allowing them to reap the consequences, and eat the bitter fruit of their own wrong choices.

God's Parenting Example

God deals with rebellion in a straightforward, honest manner. We parents would be advised to imitate His methods. Doesn't this describe the experience of many a struggling parent?

> Because I have called, and ye refused; I have stretched out my hand, and no man regarded; But ye have set at nought all my counsel, and would none of my reproof: I also will laugh at your calamity; I will mock when your fear cometh; When your fear cometh as desolation, and your destruction cometh as a whirlwind; when distress and anguish cometh upon you. . . . For that they hated knowledge, and did not choose the fear of the LORD: . . . Therefore shall they eat of the fruit of their own way, and be filled with their own devices.
>
> Proverbs 1:24–27, 29, 31

What is our job as parents? The New Testament encourages us to "bring them [our children] up in the nurture and admonition of the Lord" (Eph. 6:4).

To nurture means to further their development, to nourish them, to care for them and see that they have everything they need to grow strong and healthy. Admonition amounts to friendly reproof or counsel. That sounds like a fairly reasonable assignment, doesn't it? But what if they don't appreciate all our wonderful nurturing and don't pay the least attention to our faithful admonition?

Apparently God does not feel like a bad father if He has tried to correct and counsel His child and the child has refused to respond in obedience. He simply waits and watches, allowing the child to reap the natural consequences (the fruit) of his rebellion.

It is a parental error, and one which we will live to regret, if we continue to support our kids in their folly and to underwrite their foolishness. As long as we're leaning over the side of the ship frantically tossing lifesavers into the water, our child will never learn to swim or sink. If we want our sons and daughters to have their feet on the ground, we must put some heavy responsibility on their shoulders. Otherwise they'll never feel the burden of their foolish behavior patterns.

ALLOW YOUR CHILD
TO REAP WHAT HE OR SHE HAS SOWN

Of course, with our underage youngsters, we have to teach them principles while we lovingly protect them from catastrophic results. If you catch your three-year-old playing with matches, you're going to stamp out the fire and teach him the consequences of his wrongdoing in some way other than by allowing him to burn down the

neighborhood. But as children grow older, if we have interrupted the natural course of harvesting what has been planted, we may find that we've raised offspring who have become social parasites—who are more than happy to live off the government, friends, or a spouse. Let's release our children to failure, allow them to make their own mistakes. We've got to bite the bullet now, and pledge not to bail them out anymore—out of their filthy apartment, out of their unpaid bills, out of their overdue traffic tickets, out of their rude behavior—even out of serving an appropriate sentence in jail.

These kinds of parental decisions are not easily made. Few of us have to make a clear-cut choice between good and evil. I can remember listening to the Iran-Contra Hearings when Col. Oliver North stated,

> It's easy to make judgment calls between right and wrong. The tougher calls are the ones where you have to decide between good and better. And the worst of all are the ones where you have to decide between bad and worse.

As far as our children are concerned, it's bad to watch them "reap." But it's far worse to enable them as they develop a crippling lifestyle.

One good friend of ours, Bill, tearfully recounted to Hal and me how he had called the police to report a crime—his son was dealing drugs from his bedroom. Bill said that it was both the worst and the best night of his life. It was an agonizing experience, because his son felt that Bill had betrayed him. But it was ultimately a good decision. That heartbreaking event triggered the beginning of the end of the son's prodigal syndrome.

Because we love our own flesh and blood, it "feels" right when we cover for them, enable them, and make excuses for their offenses. But in doing so, we're simply extending their trip down the prodigal spiral. And in the process, we feel a bit self-righteous, maybe a little like godly martyrs, as we swallow the bitter fruit our kids should be tasting for themselves.

Making Ourselves Feel Better

When we find out the "bad news" about our children, the revelation usually occurs in the course of a process. We get hints, then suspicions, then the truth begins to leak out. As these things start happening, our emotions are devastated. We feel mocked by our efforts at being good parents. We feel like fools in the eyes of our friends. We feel frustrated and desperate. If we're coldly honest with ourselves, sometimes our efforts at rescuing our children are as much for our relief as for theirs.

We want them to act out the script we've written for their lives. When they don't, we try to adjust circumstances to get them back to the script as quickly as possible.

- We envision them as excellent students and responsible children, so we write dishonest notes to the teacher to excuse their incomplete homework.
- We want friends and relatives kept in the dark about their illegal activities, so we bail them out of jail so no one will find out they were arrested.
- We want them to succeed and "make us proud," so we pay their past due bills and slip them money (sometimes behind our spouse's back) so they won't "have such a struggle."

Certainly our hearts ache for them. We empathize with their shame, their sense of failure, and their inability to cope. Our motives are often mixed, and we may not even know ourselves why we do what we do. But the pattern of rescuing, enabling, and co-dependency is a dangerous one. Many counselors see it as an addictive behavior pattern, stemming from our failure to cope with our own depression, low self-esteem, or personal emptiness.

And sometimes, as Christian parents, we make the further mistake of trying to play Holy Spirit in our children's lives. We try to act out the Scripture that says, "It is the lovingkindness of God that leads us to repentance." In our efforts to see "all things work together for good," we step in and cut off the sowing/reaping process before it has a chance to teach valuable lessons.

God, of course, is loving. But God is wise enough to see the future along with the present. He would have us release our children's discipline to Him. And perhaps, if we would quiet ourselves enough to hear His voice, He just might be saying to us, "They haven't been listening to you. Why don't you give Me a chance to get their attention?"

Little Jacob was five years old and a holy terror on his "hot wheels" tricycle. He lived on a hillside, and the driveways which led to the houses surrounding his were very steep. Although the road he lived on was a dead-end, with little traffic, his mother had warned Jacob innumerable times not to ride down the neighbors' driveways into the street.

"No one can see you coming, Jacob. You're riding much too fast down those hills, and if you keep it up you're going to get hit by a car."

The problem was, the ride was wonderfully fun. Jacob and his friends were able to zoom unbelievably fast down those driveways, and the feeling of exhilaration from the high speed was irresistable. Time and again Sheila, his mom, glanced out a window just in time to see a big, happy blur flying down the side of the hill and into the street.

"Jacob!" she'd shriek. "You get in here right now!"

She spanked him. She grounded him. She refused to give him desserts. Over and over, Jacob would repent for a few weeks. But before she knew it, he was back to his old tricks again.

One day Sheila was getting groceries out of the car. She glanced up from the trunk just in time to see two things happening at once. Jacob was hurtling down the neighbors' driveway. And a car was coming.

She screamed. The car's brakes squealed. There was a thud, and she saw Jacob's little head hit the asphalt. She ran to his side in terror. His forehead was bruised and bleeding. Fortunately, he was alive—in fact, he was fully conscious.

"It was my fault, Mommy," he whimpered. "I disobeyed you."

Sheila tried to comfort the driver of the car, who was nearly hysterical. She attempted to calm herself, so violently was her body shaking, in order to drive her pale, trembling son to the emergency hospital. Mercifully, the doctor concluded that the boy was no more than bruised and very, very frightened.

There was only one permanent result from the accident. Jacob never, ever rode down a driveway on his tricycle again.

The Regret Trap

If Jacob had been seriously injured or killed, Sheila might well have spent the rest of her life in regret. She had done her very best to keep the boy from acting foolishly, but he had continued to disobey. Since he was so young, she would have thought, "I should have taken away his tricycle. We should have moved to a different street. I should have been watching him more closely right at that moment." Regret is so often the companion of the troubled parent.

No parents should allow regrets to rob them of present or future blessings. If you lament a parenting mistake you think you've made, ask God to forgive you, ask your child to forgive you, and forgive yourself. Make a fresh start at being faithful and reliable. Don't lower your standards, but examine your expectations. And above all, don't abdicate your leadership position and throw in the towel.

Faye wept as if her heart would break. In fact, it was already broken. Her words echoed the thoughts and struggles of so many parents.

"How can you turn away your own son? There he was, pounding on my bedroom window, begging to get back in. Clyde is only nineteen, and he's still battling with his drug problem. Sure, he's been abusive at times, but he really didn't mean to hit me like that. The drug rehab programs didn't work for him, and he can't get a job. My husband kicked him out of the house after he stole our TV and stereo equipment—twice. I know he sold our stuff to buy cocaine, but I want to give him another chance. It breaks my heart to watch him suffer. My husband and I are fighting over this constantly. I feel such regret over the way I brought him up. I have to help my son; after all, I'm his mother!"

Faye is partially right. Her son very much needs help. But her regrets are of no use to him, and he does not need enabling. Kids are smart. They know who the "soft" parent is, and that's the one whose shoulder they'll cry on. Faye and her husband need support and direction from other parents who have been there. It's too tough, almost impossible, to stand our ground against the onslaught of self-condemnation that invariably overwhelms us.

Are you facing this sort of situation? Help is available! There are a number of parenting support group networks across the nation that are geared to help hurting parents get tough. Many of them can be located through the national "Tough Love" organization, comprised of local support groups. In the United States, Tough Love groups can be located by checking your local telephone directory, or by calling their national information number, 800-333-1069.

Getting Ready to Give Up

It's time for enabling families to find the support they need, to make gritty decisions, and to develop a tough-love attitude. Let's pledge together that for our own emotional health, as well as for our kids', never again to:

- Replace what they've destroyed
- Cover up and lie for them
- Make excuses for their behavior
- Bail them out
- Pay their debts

Our goal, by faith, is to permit them to reap what they sow. With God's help, it just may facilitate a swift return from their prodigal wanderings. In the meantime, there is a letting go that must take place—we'll talk about that more in the next chapter. But here are some wonderful words from Barbara Johnson to prepare us to release our sons and daughters into the hands of their heavenly Father.

There are several steps we all go through when we try to give a problem completely to God. You take your first step when life rises up to knock you flat—you CHURN. You feel as if your insides are full of knives, chopping you up in a grinder. . . .

Your next step is to BURN. That's right, you want to kill your child, and then you want to kill yourself. You are so full of red hot anger and the anguish of frustration that your temper is out of control. You literally feel as if you're burning up inside.

In your third step, you YEARN. Oh, you want so much for things to change! You just ache inside for things to be the way they were before you knew about this. You yearn for the happy past, and this stage often lasts the longest of all.

But then you take your next step, which is to LEARN. You talk with others, maybe you find a support group, and you learn that you're in a long growth process. You become more understanding and compassionate. Spiritual values you learned in the past will suddenly become *real* to you.

And, finally, you take your last step—you TURN. You learn to turn the problem over to the Lord completely by saying, "Whatever, Lord! Whatever You bring into my life, You are big enough to get me through it."

Now you can relinquish your heaviness to God, knowing that He is in control. . . . When you nail your problem to the foot of the Cross and say you have deposited that problem with the Lord and truly mean it, then you will be relieved of your crushing burden.

Giving our children up to God—what could be more right, and yet more difficult? Why is it we don't trust His wisdom enough to entrust our precious children, their choices *and* their consequences, their sowing and their reaping, into His mighty hand? We may think we know best. Perhaps, at times, we do. But no matter how strongly we feel, even when it comes to our sons and daughters, we don't really have all the answers all the time. We can't see the outcome. We cannot imagine the beautiful, new reality God may yet bring out of our shattered dreams.

As Ruth Bell Graham so eloquently wrote in *Sitting by My Laughing Fire,*

> Had I been Joseph's mother
> I'd have prayed
> protection from his brothers:
> "God keep him safe;
> he is so young,
> so different from the others."
> Mercifully she never knew
> there would be slavery
> And prison, too.
>
> Had I been Moses' mother
> I'd have wept
> to keep my little son,
> praying she might forget
> the babe drawn from the water
> of the Nile,
> had I not kept
> him for her
> nursing him the while?
> Was he not mine
> and she
> but Pharoah's daughter?
>
> Had I been Daniel's mother
> I should have pled,
> "Give victory!
> This Babylonian horde—
> godless and cruel—
> don't let them take him captive
> —better dead,
> Almighty Lord!

Had I been Mary—
Oh, had I been she,
I would have cried
as never mother cried,
". . . Anything, O God,
anything . . .
but crucified!"

With such prayers
importunate,
my finite wisdom
would assail
Infinite Wisdom;

God, how fortunate
Infinite Wisdom
should prevail.

8

Letting Go

A Tranquilizer for Frazzled Nerves

As children bring their broken toys
    with tears for us to mend,
I brought my broken dreams to God
    because He was my friend.
But then, instead of leaving Him
    in peace to work alone,
I hung around and tried to help
    with ways that were my own.
At last, I snatched them back and cried,
    "How can you be so slow?"
"My child," He said, "what could I do?
    You never did let go."

Source Unknown

Let Nature Take Its Course

Marlene, a friend of ours, tells the story of her brief encounter with an injured sandpiper. Marlene lives near a broad stretch of California beach, and on one of her summer walks along the water she came upon a broken, battered sea bird. His body was severely pecked and bloodied, and he lay limp in the sand at the edge of the water.

The beach has a lifeguard station, but it is quite a long walk from where she found the sandpiper. Thinking that a lifeguard might be able to contact some sort of animal control center, Marlene lifted the soggy creature into her arms and headed for the lifeguard.

At first the bird was still, and she wondered if it wasn't about to die. After a few minutes' walk, however, it began to stir and struggle a little. Marlene held it tightly, noticing two dogs on the beach that would have probably enjoyed having it for lunch.

Again it dozed, then woke up, more abruptly this time. It struggled between her fingers, and did something impolite in her hands, which she didn't appreciate at all.

"Be still," she growled at the panicky bird. "I'm trying to help you."

The pattern continued. Dozing and struggling, stillness and frantic wrestling. The bird seemed to be getting stronger, somehow, but its bedraggled condition had convinced Marlene that she simply couldn't leave it to fate— it desperately needed an appointment with a bird doctor.

"Will you stop fighting me? I'm trying to save your life, you stupid bird!"

At last she reached the lifeguard. He took one look at her sweaty face and earnest expression and concluded that she was some sort of crazed animal rights activist. He asked, "What am I supposed to do with it?"

Marlene snapped back. "Well, what am I supposed to do with it? Let it die?"

"Let it go," he shrugged. "Let nature take its course."

She was disgusted with the young man's disinterest in the injured creature. She was also less than pleased with the condition of her hands, which by now had been severely pecked and otherwise abused. Meanwhile, although the bird was dozing again, she realized it would begin its angry struggling any second. "No point in taking it home," she reasoned. "I'll just have to leave it."

Marlene carried the bird to the edge of the water. She set it on the sand. It tried to stand up several times, but immediately fell over on its side. When it did find its footing, it spun around and around, finally falling, beak first, into the wet sand. Marlene would have laughed, but she had the sinking feeling that the sandpiper was about to drown in the Pacific Ocean. It all seemed rather tragic, particularly when she thought about the valiant efforts she'd personally made to rescue it.

Marlene had two alternatives, and the only one that made sense was to walk away and leave the bird. She turned her back just as it spun around and crashed on its side for the tenth time. She looked back twice more. It appeared to be brain damaged, lost in a drunken stupor. But the third time she turned to look, she stopped in her tracks, transfixed. The bird was flapping its wings, trying to run, careening, reeling. It fell, then got up, then fell again.

Suddenly, the injured sandpiper rose into the air. And before Marlene could catch her breath it was flying—soaring as if nothing was wrong with it, higher and higher, until it disappeared in the sky.

Life presents many problems. Some are challenges that carry us to great heights of inspiration. Others are seemingly hopeless difficulties that exhaust our resources, drain our emotions and leave us feeling as if God, despite His promises, has "left us and forsaken us." Inevitably we reach a point where there's simply nothing further we can do. At that strategic moment, there's one common prescription, meant to tranquilize us. The prescription can be summed up in two very important words:

LET GO!

Solo Flights, Crash Landings

The story is told of an agnostic who was working on the roof of his house. Unexpectedly he slipped, and he found himself dangling from the drainpipe. He strained his neck to look up and cried, "Is there anybody up there?"

A booming voice filled the sky with: "Trust in God and let go."

After a moment of silent contemplation, the fellow replied, "Is there anybody *else* up there?"

That story describes more about us parents than we'd dare to admit. When troubles bear down around us and our emotions scream at us to "act before it's too late," quiet faith seems unrealistic. God seems like a distant, disinterested unknown. And His Word sounds like a collection of happy thoughts.

Most of us can do pretty much anything except let go and trust God. We often find ourselves saying, "If He's really there and He really cares, *why doesn't He do something?*"

Hal and I are bird lovers, and we've learned some things from our feathered friends. Marlene's story reminds me of a period when our family raised small birds—finches of all kinds. They were a joy to watch in the aviary just off the kitchen window. After their eggs hatched, the struggling new family would be crammed into one little nesting box—very crowded quarters.

Through some mysterious determination known only to them, at an appointed time Mom and Dad Bird concluded that it was time for the kids to leave the nest. At this point they began to make the Bird household very uncomfortable for the offspring.

Trusting little birdlings, who had never known anything but gentle care and protection from the parents, were now being pushed out through a small hole and forced to face a cruel world. They didn't have the slightest idea how to use their wings, and it was somewhat comical to watch them trying out this new and hazardous flying activity.

As the baby birds grappled for independence they invariably flew in the wrong direction and almost knocked themselves unconscious on the kitchen window. Dazed but determined, they'd shake themselves and try again. Occasionally the little ones would pair up with the wrong buddies and get pecked and scorned. How painful it must have been for the parents to watch all this, knowing if they rescued their babies, they would never develop the strength needed to survive.

Deep Roots, Strong Wings

During this learning period, I embroidered a popular saying, and hung it in our bedroom as a reminder:

**THERE ARE TWO LASTING THINGS
WE CAN GIVE OUR CHILDREN:
ONE IS ROOTS—
THE OTHER IS WINGS!**

Once the roots are firmly implanted, the wings must be allowed to grow and stretch and allow our children to fly. This letting go process means we have to relinquish, surrender rights to, and give up claim to our children.

When it comes to releasing our children to God so they can live out their own lives, one parental malady we need to avoid is something we might call a hardening of the attitudes; an affliction which affects both moms and pops. There are three necessary antidotes to this hardening, which need to be applied in equal dosage:

```
FAITH, TRUST, AND HOPE
```

We have been chief decision makers for so long, it's tough to learn how to "abdicate" gracefully—to permit a peaceful exchange of power, and allow our child the inevitable privilege of becoming an adult. These words may encourage you as you consider releasing your own sons and daughters.

LETTING GO

To let go doesn't mean to STOP CARING
    it means I can't DO IT for someone else.
To let go is not to CUT MYSELF OFF,
    it's the realization that I can't CONTROL
    another.
To let go is not to ENABLE,
    but to allow learning from natural
    CONSEQUENCES.
To let go is to admit POWERLESSNESS, which
    means
    the OUTCOME is not in MY hands.
To let go is not to try to CHANGE or BLAME
    another,
    I can only change myself.
To let go is not to CARE FOR, but to care
    ABOUT.
To let go is not to FIX, but to be SUPPORTIVE.
To let go is not to JUDGE, but to allow another
    to be a human being.
To let go is not to be in the MIDDLE, arranging
    all the outcomes, but to ALLOW others to
    EFFECT their own outcomes.

To let go is not to be PROTECTIVE,
   it is to allow another to FACE REALITY.
To let go is not to DENY, but to ACCEPT.
To let go is not to NAG, SCOLD or ARGUE, but
   to SEARCH OUT MY OWN
   SHORTCOMINGS and correct them.
To let go is not to ADJUST everything to my
   desires,
   but to take each day as it comes, and to
   CHERISH the moment.
To let go is not to CRITICIZE or REGULATE
   anyone
   but to become the BEST I CAN BE.
To let go is not to REGRET the past,
   but to GROW today and PREPARE for the
   future.
To let go is to FEAR LESS, trust in Christ more,
   and freely give to others the love He's given
   to me.

                                        Source Unknown

**LEARN THE SECRET
OF LETTING GO
AND LETTING GOD!**

Mothering, Not Smothering

Just like Mr. and Mrs. Bird, we may feel distress as we observe our little ones practicing their independence. But just as the unborn child cannot stay in the womb, the teenager must one day exit the safety and security of our watchful eye. And it's a given that they'll fly with the wrong crowd and in the wrong direction once in a while. Occasionally they'll drag themselves home, bruised and battered. Although we can't rescue them, it is our job to give encouragement and inspiration as they practice using their wings.

Poet and songwriter Gloria Gaither reminds us:

> It always calms the storm of parental worry to know that God loves our children infinitely more than we can, because He is the perfect parent with perfect love. I am able to be with and help my children only to the limit of my presence. But there is no boundary to His presence.

We may laugh at the stereotypical "Jewish Mama" who is clinging and possessive of her child. But let's be honest. Every parent has the inherent potential for suffocating her child, for being overprotective and overpossessive. Isn't it time we surrendered the need to be needed, and the habits that make our children feel emotionally bound to us?

As our children grow, the power of our influence over them should be diminishing:

	Parents' Influence	Child's Responsibility
Age 5	95%	5%
Age 14	65%	35%
Age 19	5%	95%

Too many emotionally crippled college students are wandering around campus unable to make career path decisions. You can spot one now and then, pitifully holding his umbilical cord, pleading, "Where do I plug this thing in?" These overage dependents verify the fact that a child cannot gain his freedom from a parent until the parent gains his freedom from the child.

Part of the problem lies with mothers who are desperate to have their own "love needs" supplied, which compels them to keep their children dependent. This is not only unhealthy for both parents and children, but it has a counter-effect: grasping only serves to alienate.

Working ourselves out of a job—that is our assignment! We are to strive to relinquish our parental control. It's difficult, but vital, for us to learn to trust God with our kids and let go of our death grip . . .

- On the first day of school
- For an overnight stay at a friend's house
- With the ex-spouse
- With grandparents
- With baby-sitters

One friend of mine recalls having to give up her newborn son to God before they ever left the maternity hospital. "I was deathly afraid of Sudden Infant Death Syndrome," she told me. "And the very first day I held my first baby in my arms I was almost afraid to touch him. I'd never felt that kind of love before. What if he died? I remember saying, 'I'll just have to give him to you Lord, because he's so precious I'm almost too scared to take care of him.'"

Of course, very few creatures are as helpless as newborn humans. But, as the kids grow, it is healthy to implement the policy of "do nothing for your child which he can profit in doing for himself." Sometimes, when this seems unfair, it helps to remind them, "I won't always be around to help you out. Someday you'll be buying your own clothes, cooking your own meals, washing your own laundry." It is not always easy to visualize our babies as adults, but that's where they're headed, with or without our cooperation.

Instead, we tend to hold on too tightly, long after it is appropriate. Let's remind ourselves that we have a responsibility to stop being a "smothering mother" and to become a "significant other."

PARENT:
MOVE FROM OMNIPOTENT ONE
TO SIGNIFICANT OTHER

They Must Increase, We Must Decrease

As I've read my Bible, I've noted something fascinating about how Jesus handled the "letting go" process with His disciples. When the disciples were young and inexperienced, Jesus instructed them before a journey:

> Don't even take along a walking stick . . . nor a beggar's bag, nor food, nor money. Not even an extra coat!
>
> Luke 9:3 TLB

But as they were growing, Jesus revised His instructions:

> When I sent you out to preach the Good News and you were without money, duffle bag, or extra clothing, how did you get along?
> "Fine," they replied.
> But now . . . take a duffle bag if you have one, and your money. And if you don't have a sword, better sell your clothes and buy one!
>
> Luke 22:35–36 TLB

Hey, what's this about a sword? Jesus had always protected them; He'd done everything for them. But now, it was time to for them to grow up, to be responsible. Now He was instructing them to provide, to some extent, their own physical protection.

Rebellion, which is bad news, seems to be a necessary part of the independence process, which is good news. So allow your child, gradually, to "rebel" in areas which aren't all that important anyway, such as bedtime, clothes, hair, or tidiness.

In a letter to me, Darlene Cunningham, director of the University of the Nations in Kona, Hawaii (and wife of Youth with a Mission's Loren Cunningham), made some interesting observations about youthful rebellion. She spoke of how it is easy for us to excuse a naughty two-year-old, citing the "terrible twos." We recognize that he is determined to prove his separateness by doing the total opposite of what is requested. Then she states,

> It is my personal conviction that as they come into their teen years, they are forced to go through something like the "terrible twos" in order to gain recognition as their own person with a separate identity from their parents. . . . And parents can label a child as rebellious who wants to wear way-out clothes, strange hairdos, and too many earrings. In truth, he is just wanting to be recognized as somebody different and separate from his parents. The wise parent won't make this into an issue. Don't sweat the small stuff—save your influence for the truly big issues. Our children ARE to be separate people from us. Our role is to give them a proper value system based on God's word and equip them with tools for making their own decisions.

During trying times, a parent can better survive life with a "terrible teen-ager" by offering him responsibility, trust, and lots of space. During this period kids may test you with startling comments—just to get a rise out of you.

"I'm leaving to live with my boyfriend."

"I'm signing up for the Army."

"How do you know if you have VD?"

"How can you tell if you're gay?"

"What happens if you get caught shoplifting?"

"I'm thinking about hitchhiking across the country."

Smile bravely, answer calmly and keep telling yourself:

> ### THIS, TOO, SHALL PASS.

One sure way to instigate or prolong rebellion is to hold on tightly to your children—it will drive them toward staking out their own territory. A child who is too tightly controlled will feel compelled to prove that his parents don't pull all the strings on behavior. It is actually unhealthy for a child to accept his parents' domination compliantly and without a fight.

> ### REBELLION: THE CONTRACTIONS OF A NEW BIRTH OF FREEDOM!

To Love Is to Set Free

The Bible chronicles the story of two women who were both claiming to be the birth mother of the same infant. So King Solomon put them to the ultimate test. Here's how the Bible records the story:

> Then the king said, . . . "Bring me a sword.
> . . . Divide the living child in two and give half to each of these women!"
> Then the woman who really was the mother of the child, and who loved him very much, cried out,

"Oh, no, sir! Give her the child—don't kill him."

But the other woman said, "All right, it will be neither yours nor mine; divide it between us!"

Then the king said, "Give the baby to the woman who wants him to live, for she is the mother!"

1 Kings 3:23–27

Perhaps we can interpret this story for ourselves like this: authentic parents must learn to let a child go, in order for him to live. Children cannot be divided between their own ownership and ours. We have to come to grips with the understanding that our children are not our own; they are on loan from the Lord.

As you let go and let God take over the parenting role, you'll discover that as you let go of what's in your hand, God will let go of what is in His hand.

> **IF YOU LOVE SOMETHING,
> LET IT GO. IF IT RETURNS TO YOU,
> IT WAS YOURS; IF IT DOESN'T,
> IT NEVER WAS.**

Letting Go of What?

Sometimes it's difficult for us to see just exactly how and why we're holding on. We may crave being in control. We may want to protect. We may long to provide. We feel we have released our kids in most areas, and yet we have a feeling that in some ways we're still hanging on to some aspect of them for dear life. Here are a few ways parents can keep "hands off."

- *Let Go of the Enforcer Role.* Let's accept the fact that we cannot be omnipresent. Remember that there is Someone more powerful than ourselves to whom we can release our kids. Parents can only be the "conviction factor" for so long.

- *Let Go of the Terminator Role.* Let's turn in our badges as our children's personal parole officer, warden, and executioner. The threatening role must come to an end.

- *Let Go of Anger.* We may be justified; it may be warranted. But let's make the choice to set aside the multipurpose use of our anger and becoming forgiving parents.

- *Let Go of Their Bad Track Record.* Let's determine to start fresh, with new insights we have received; we are putting their failures behind us. Let's begin choosing to recall the good things, their strengths, their sensitivities, their special gifts.

- *Let Go of False Hopes.* Can you pledge not to put your faith in another magic moment—a new friend, a new school, a new outfit? Forget the "if onlys" and the "somedays." Once we reduce our expectations, we will not be so deeply disappointed again.

- *Let Go of Damages Due You.* Let's cancel any "emotional debt" our child owes us because we "gave him the best years of our lives." Our care for him will no longer be a deposit in our old-age care-due-us account. This will enable us to stop requiring our children to return home on occasions that are special to us. We will no longer hold their emotional feet to the fire until they pay back what they owe.

Prayer of Release

I often rent cars when I travel. Recently I was returning a car at the airport. Just as I dropped off the keys, I realized this ordinary event is much like what God expects us to do with our kids. Once they're raised, we need to return them to Him. By an act of our parental wills, we have to let go of our claim to our sons and daughters.

Are you ready to give up, let go, and set free your children? If so, take a moment to fill in their names as you pray this prayer of release.

Dear Father God,

Thank You for my children, _____. I acknowledge that they were Your idea, and I received them from Your Hand to be meant as a blessing. Now, as a parent, I let go of my claim to ownership of my children and ask You to forgive my stumbling ways in parenting.

When I receive any conviction of sin from You, I will repent and do whatever is necessary to rectify the problem. But I reject any guilt, accusation, and condemnation that Satan, our mutual enemy, would want to put on my family. In the name of Jesus Christ, I break any evil power that would seek to hinder _____.

I believe You are not willing that _____ should perish, but have everlasting life. I pray for a spirit of repentance to overtake _____. Convince him/her that he/she can still be a part of the plan You have for his/her life.

I ask that You would deliver my children from evil and give them every opportunity to turn back to You. I also ask You to apply whatever pressure it takes to effect that change.

With faith in Christ, I cling to the hope of Your divine intervention in _____'s life. Grant me the peace and hope to endure and see Your will come to pass Your way, and in Your time.

In Jesus' name, Amen.

9

Taking Hold

A Tonic for Daily Strength

Most Mother's Day cards are pretty mushy and sentimental. But the one I like the best has a couple of far-out, punk teen-agers on it—wild hairdos, black leather, and all. It simply states:

> Mom, you should have KNOWN
> I'd be hard to raise . . .
> even before I was BORN
> I made you throw up!

Parenting could be described in one word: persistence. It means you are there when your kids don't want you there. It's the only job in the world where you get fired regularly, and the people you're sworn to serve tell you, "Leave me alone."

> BE NICE TO YOUR CHILDREN . . .
> THEY WILL SOMEDAY CHOOSE
> YOUR REST HOME

While we are letting go of some of our hurts and the mistaken mindsets that may have caused our pain, let's also take hold of a few important precepts. Let's swallow some of God's parenting megavitamins, which promise to strengthen us, build our faith, and bolster our hope.

Take Hold of the Present

Parents who find themselves needing Emotional Intensive Care may have a tendency to focus on either the past or the future. Past-fixated parents are always groaning:

"If only we'd sent Barkley to Christian school, he wouldn't have gotten into all this trouble."

"We shouldn't have moved when we did."

"I shouldn't have been so tough on her while she was growing up."

"Why did I let him spend so many weekends with his father?"

Future-fixated parents spend alot of time and energy dreaming of how good it's going to be someday or conjuring up frightening scenarios that may never happen.

"What if she gets pregnant?"

"If we can just get him through high school, he'll straighten out."

"When he lands a decent job . . ."

"Suppose he gets thrown in jail and I have to bail him out?"

As a soul-strengthening tonic, we need to abandon both wishful and wistful thinking and begin to live in the now. Let's place our faith in God and His ability to make the best of the past, His ability to give to us a future more wonderful than we could ask or think. Today is the only day we have been given to live—yesterday is a memory, tomorrow is a dream. As Jesus said, "Each day has enough trouble of its own." Sometimes we overlook a day's greatest blessings by dwelling on the past or the future and letting some present delight pass us by.

Take Hold of Responsibilities

Another way of increasing our parenting stamina is to learn to face up to the things for which we have been given responsibility. We shouldn't "stuff" our perplexing feelings any more. If we have genuine sense of guilt for a specific parenting failure and feel we are to blame for some of it, that's OK. Face the facts, consider the present circumstances, and deal with the issue.

While you are not assuming the responsibility FOR your child's destiny, you may well have blown it in the responsible TO category. Resist this general "I don't know what I've done, but there must be something" feeling and begin to confess specific failures or transgressions. If you can't think of any, let the feeling go—it's false guilt. If you do have to face some faults, 1 John 1:9 encourages that "if we confess our sins, he is faithful and just to forgive us our sins, and to cleanse us from all unrighteousness."

Confess the parental failings:

To God—He may be waiting to hear you admit it.

To yourself—you are receiving conviction of wrongdoing.

To your child—be specific in recalling a time
you felt you really blew it.

Ask forgiveness and wait for a response.

The twelve-step recovery programs talk about making amends as part of our efforts to get our lives back on
track. There may be times when we have to make amends
to our kids. Our friend Paul recently went through this
process with his daughters. He explained to them that he
had been going through a spiritual renewal. He said that
he had become more aware of the realm of spiritual war-
fare, and that he had been asking God to help him re-
claim some things he might have lost along the way.

"Maybe you've been through some things," he tearfully explained to her, "because I haven't been the kind of
spiritual leader I should have been."

"Let's make a list of issues we need to discuss, he sug-
gested. You make your list, and I'll make mine. Then we'll
get together again—if we can't find a way to resolve them,
we'll get a third party to help us."

One specific area in which this dad felt he needed to
"make amends" regarded keeping control over the girls'
adult lives. He is a strong-willed man, and it had become
clear to him that he had been overly domineering with his
daughters.

One daughter commented, "You know, Dad, you always told us that God has a plan for our lives. Don't you
think he has my phone number so He can call me and He
won't have to call you first?"

"You're right. He does, and from now on I've got nothing to do with your relationship with God. You and I
should be adult friends. We'll always be father and daughter. But now it's time to commit ourselves to friendship for
the rest of our lives."

Take Hold of Your Feelings

This kind of openness is one way we can "walk in the light," then "we have fellowship" with each other (1 John 1:7). Exposing your negative feelings to the light is so healthy. It's been said that we're only as sick as our secrets, and emotional secrets are unhealthy. Depressing and defeating thoughts tend to grow in the dark like sinister mushrooms. But when they are brought out into the light, they shrink to their proper size.

It's important for you to accept the fact that your feelings of disappointment, disillusionment, and discouragement are not *wrong;* they just *are.* Feelings are not wrong or right; they are amoral. "Be angry and sin not" is Scripture that applies here. The feeling of anger is involuntary. We are only responsible for how we deal with that anger.

Some people find it easier to cope with their emotions when they keep a daily diary. Writing in a journal helps us shine the light on hidden issues. It's sort of like treating diaper rash—when you take off the diaper and put the baby's bare bottom in the sunshine, the rash heals. So it is with directing light onto our emotions. Keeping a diary helps air out parenting wounds, allowing them to heal.

Take Hold of a Positive Attitude

The Bible also has some good things to say about the thoughts we keep in our minds. In Philippians we read,

> Finally, brothers, whatever is true, whatever is noble, whatever is right, whatever is pure, whatever is lovely, whatever is admirable—if anything is excellent or praiseworthy—think about such things.
>
> Philippians 4:8 NIV

Recently, I saw an old acquaintance. I knew she had an estranged, prodigal daughter, and after exchanging niceties, I asked, "What is your daughter up to these days?"

This positive mom replied, in sheer faith, "Oh, she's out building her testimony!"

What a relief it is to center on the positive and eliminate the negative in our thoughts toward our kids. Recall the joys you've had in parenting, the good memories, the photo albums, the treasures and trophies. The happy times have clearly been there, and we don't want to forget even a moment of the love and satisfaction we have shared with our children.

And, besides enjoying pleasant memories, why not lighten up today? With all the heavy things we deal with, and considering all the stresses on our lives, we need to learn to laugh at our troubles, at our foolish mistakes, and, mostly, at ourselves.

Arvella Schuller, wife of the Crystal Cathedral's Dr. Bob Schuller and mother of five, recalls a healing incident during a painful period:

> When my thirteen-year-old, Carol, came home from her hospital stay, after having her leg amputated, her stump was bandaged, and she was in a wheelchair. The chair wouldn't go through the bathroom door, so I tried to help her. We both toppled over, and hit the floor a tangled mess of bandages, legs, arms, and clothes. Carol, in a great deal of pain, started to cry, and I (in a helpless state) soon joined her in a loud, long duet on the bathroom floor.
>
> When we finally quieted down, we looked at each other and began to laugh! We knew we had to solve this by ourselves. Released first by tears, then by laughter, we were again ready to creatively solve our dilemma. We can be encouraged through the healing power of a good loud cry, followed by a good loud laugh . . . at ourselves!

As we attempt to lighten up, we may need to alter our habit of complaining about the kids to our friends. We also may need to get input from more positive influences than our usual group of associates. Let's take whatever steps are necessary to become more upbeat people!

Take Hold of Faith and Keep It!

You're doing all you can to take hold of life with both hands, including building up your emotional strength with some good mental exercises. But it's even more important for you to give yourself extra courage and stamina by bolstering your faith. You can do this by counting on the promises of God, and by trusting Him to intervene.

If your faith has been shaken through your strenuous parenting ordeal, that is understandable. However, our troubles aren't meant to shake our faith, but rather to diminish our reliance upon our own resources. As we grow in a personal faith with Jesus, our faith can actually become the "substance" of the things we hope for.

Before Billy Graham's prodigal son Franklin returned to the Lord, his mother, Ruth, reported slipping to her knees and committing her son, again, to the Lord. Ruth says, "God impressed me with 'You take care of the possible, and trust Me for the impossible.'"

On the day of Franklin's ordination, Ruth rejoiced as a still, small voice reminded her, "Today you are seeing the impossible!"

A MOTHER'S COVERS
When you were small and just a touch away,
I covered you with blankets on a winter's day.
But now that you're big, and hardly ever there,
I fold my hands, my child,
and I cover you with prayer.

Reach out for Christ's hand in your situation; His hands are not tied. They are reaching out to us saying, "Put that disappointment in my Hands. I did not cause this harm to happen to you, but I am the only One who can turn evil into good."

Take Hold Through Prayer

The old adage "prayer changes things" could also read "prayer changes people." Not only does prayer change the hearts of the people we pray for, it changes us, too. And God will begin preparing the answer as we begin to pray FOR people, not AT them. Pray for the dissipation of the spiritual blindness that surrounds them, and for their healing from the poisons of our sin-sick world.

The bad news about prayer is that sometimes the answers are rather slow in coming. "In his time," the Bible explains, "He makes all things beautiful in his time." But the good news about prayer is that it works! Entertainer Pat Boone told me the following story:

> In parenting we didn't bat a thousand, but we were on our knees continually, praying for our four daughters. Once, when our daughter Debby and I were having a major disagreement, her sister Cherry told Debby she had walked into our bedroom one night and discovered me on my knees, praying for Debby out loud, and in tears. When Debby heard this, it had a great impact on her, and our relationship changed right then.
>
> My wife, Shirley, and I can gratefully testify that God did deliver our girls from the maze of Beverly Hills temptations, to their wedding partners untouched by drugs and promiscuity. If that can happen for parents in Hollywood, we have faith for parents anywhere!

Take Hold in Your Marriage

If you are married, refuse to let the problems with children cause injury to your primary relationship with your spouse. None of us should let our parenting pain divide us from our husbands or wives, alienate us from God, or keep us from being a help to others. If you are a single parent, these same parenting problems have the power to stir up arguments with your relatives and close friends. If you are a stepparent, guard against the child pitting you against the "real" parent, which can create another set of very unpleasant circumstances.

Get some insurance against these storms with a "No Separation" policy with your spouse. Kids know parenting disagreements have the power to alienate a mom and dad. If they get the idea that they can drive a wedge between their parents they will play on it to their advantage. Your child's defiance is a threat to the unity of the entire family; it can divide the other children as well. Guard against it.

> ### PLEDGE A NO SEPARATION POLICY

It isn't unusual for one parent to be labeled the "yes" parent, and one the "no." It doesn't take kids long to figure out who the softy is, and this identification alone can cause a breach between parents. Some experts tell us that in many cases it is more important for the parents be united than for them to be infallibly right. The kids benefit by seeing the strength of your togetherness.

Before this gap begins to widen, discuss this issue with your spouse. Talk it out. Express to each other what you feel, think, and need. Many times, Dad thinks of these struggles as simply "a phase," while Mom feels something is terribly wrong. Either one could be right, so it's essential to communicate.

Take Hold of Helping Hands

When you're trying to discipline yourself in a new exercise program, it's a lot easier to stick with it when you have a room full of people to keep you motivated. That's why aerobics classes are so much more fun than Jane Fonda tapes in your den (unless you can't bear to be seen in your leotard).

As you continue to build yourself up, getting strong and fit, you'll find that supportive friends, other than your spouse, may be needed. Why not seek out other parents who are enduring the same pain as you? Author Barbara Johnson conducts numerous parent support groups where people find invaluable assurance and assistance. Barb calls her outreach program Spatula Ministries—because she is always scraping some parent off the ceiling!

"Isolation kills," Barbara advises. This wise mom, who is author of the bestseller *Stick a Geranium in Your Hat and Be Happy!* has had her fair share of parenting pain.

"Simply sitting alone, reading your Bible and praying, doesn't cut it. Find a support group! We cry on each other's shoulders, listen to our mutual war stories, encourage ourselves with tapes, and claim the promises of God for the healing of our children, and our own distress."

Remember, although God has not brought these problems upon you, He stands with you in the midst of them. He is anxious for this period to come to an end. After all, He is more concerned for your child than you are; He has a plan for your child's life, and longs to see it fulfilled.

Twelve Steps for Parents in Pain

Some of us may feel that our kids are driving us to drink—let's hope that's not the literal truth. But those who are recovering from drinking problems have learned a great deal about God, themselves, and their relationships with others. One of the most helpful methods for recovery is the twelve-step program, based on the Alcoholics Anonymous *Big Book*. Although the original twelve steps are intended to deal with substance addiction, they can be easily adapted to accommodate the needs of parents who are trying to recover from their endless battle with pain.

Step One. *Admit that you are powerless to control and think for your children, and that whenever you've tried to play God in their lives, the situation has become unmanageable.* Of course, when children are small, we must take authority over their behavior and must teach them principles of healthy thinking. But as our sons and daughters grow, we must release them from our control. And, as far too many parents have learned, even when we seem to have done everything "right," things can become pretty unmanageable anyway.

Step Two. *Accept the fact that God is the only one who can restore you to sanity.* God is all-powerful, all-wise, and everywhere at once. We are none-of-the-above, no matter how we try. God, along with His power, is also a caring parent whose heart aches over our plight as struggling moms and dads. It is His choice to have us "cast every care on Him."

Step Three. *Make a decision to turn your will and your concerns for your children over to God.* You already know that "God reigns," but somehow you may be trying to hang on to the controls anyway. You have many dreams, hopes, and yearnings for your children, as do all loving parents. Beautiful as those thoughts may be, it's time to give them up. Instead of telling God what you want Him to do, practice praying the simple prayer of Jesus, "*Thy will be done.*"

Step Four. *Make a soul-searching examination of yourself as a parent.* Get rid of vague anxieties and guilt feelings by confronting both your strengths and your weaknesses. It's important to ask the Holy Spirit to bring to your mind anything He would have you remember. And it's also wise to ask the Lord to help you hear His voice and no other. During a process like this, Satan, who is sometimes called "the accuser of the brethren," steps in and whispers condemning thoughts in our ears. Ask the Lord to keep him silent as you seek truth about yourself as a parent.

Step Five. *Admit to God, to yourself, and to another human being the exact nature of your past mistakes, your parental weaknesses, and your inadequacies.* It's important to share your new understanding of yourself with a trusted friend. First of all, you won't be so quick to make the same mistakes again. But, in an equally important way, it also keeps you from being too hard on yourself. Because they are capable of objectivity and perspective which we lack, friends can give us a more balanced view of our circumstances than we are able to provide for ourselves.

Step Six. *Prepare yourself to take your failures to God, while giving up your perfectionism and unreasonable expectations.* It's good to take a little time with your fact-finding endeavors. Sometimes, after a good night's sleep and some helpful conversation with a friend, we see things from a different perspective. Preparing ourselves isn't an endless process of procrastination. It is, instead, a reasonable amount of time to collect our thoughts, evaluate our motives, and plan our strategies for future change.

Step Seven. *Humbly confess your parenting faults and failures to the Lord, asking for forgiveness and that He will remove your shortcomings.* True repentance, of course, means turning and going in the opposite direction. This seventh step is a step of repentance. Even though we know that we may fail again, it is important for us to ask God's forgiveness. And, as we've already realized, He is the only one who can really change us— from the inside out.

Step Eight. *Make a list of the things you may have done to injure or disappoint your children, preparing yourself to make whatever amends are necessary.* Sometimes this process of preparing to make amends finds us saying, "Yes, but look what they did to me!" A forgiving spirit is vital here—and while you're at it, be sure you remember to forgive yourself, just as the Lord has forgiven you. Preparing to make amends means weighing the possibilities of how our conversations may help others. The AA making amends step reads, Let's plan to face up to the way we've done harm "except when to do so would injure them or others."

Step Nine. *Make amends to your children for the past through conversation, improved performance, and any restitution you may feel is necessary.* During this process it's important to remember not to overcompensate, which is always a temptation when we're really sorry for something we've done to a person we dearly love. As we make amends with our children, since we will be spending the rest of our lives with them, it is wise to focus on enjoying better tomorrows rather than mourning unhappy yesterdays.

Step Ten. *Keeping your past patterns in mind, stay on top of your behavior, and quickly deal with relapses into old, unhealthy habits.* The older we get, the more entrenched our habits have become. Nobody's perfect, and we're bound to backslide now and then as we try to form better relationships with our sons and daughters. Don't expect perfection of yourself, or of your children. On the other hand, don't hesitate to get back on track.

Step Eleven. *Seek a closer relationship with God, and ask Him to reveal His will to you.* As you draw closer to Him, try to model a more godly life for your children, bearing in mind that they have to make their own spiritual choices. Don't allow their rejection of your religious culture or even your Christian values separate you from them as friends. Remember, as the Scripture says, "Love covers a multitude of sins."

Step Twelve. *Reach out to other parents in the spirit of mutual support and compassion.* Building a strong support system will enable you to weather storms of your own, as well as provide a strong arm to others who may be in pain.

And with step twelve in mind, let's remember the beautiful prayer of St. Francis of Assisi, praying it for ourselves as we consider our children and the deep love we hold in our hearts for them.

> Lord, make me an instrument of Thy peace!
> Where there is hatred—let met sow love
> Where there is injury—pardon
> Where there is doubt—faith
> Where there is despair—hope
> Where there is darkness—light
> Where there is sadness—joy.
> O Divine Master, grant that I may not so much
>   seek
> To be consoled—as to console
> To be understood—as to understand
> To be loved—as to love.

For it is in giving—that we receive
It is in pardoning—that we are pardoned
It is in dying—that we are born to eternal life.

10

Here's to Your Health!

A Lifetime Supply of Peace

PICTURE AN INNER CITY AREA with graffiti on the walls, homeless people wandering on the sidewalks, and rubbish in the gutter. Sure enough, here comes a would-be preacher in a long, white robe, toting a large sign with bold lettering: "Repent: The End of the World Is at Hand."

If I were to follow behind him, my placard would read:

> THE END IS *NOT* NEAR;
> YOU MUST LEARN TO COPE!

It's quite important for us to realize that "the end," as parents, is not just around the corner of a long and winding road. In fact, parenting brings a sobering new meaning to the phrase "until death do us part." As moms and dads in pain, our goal is not to "get it over with," but to cope—to survive, successfully, a godly assignment that is both challenging and rewarding. God expects us to deal with our difficulties and emerge as healthy, whole people.

We Can Count on God's Forgiveness

We know from His Word that despite our failures and foolishness, the Father still loves us as His own kids. Naturally, He loves our sons and daughters just the way He loves us. So how does He feel when the actions of one of His children speak louder than His well-intentioned words? Does the Divine Father simply shrug His shoulders in disinterest? No, the Scriptures paint God as deeply feeling, full of emotion. But what kind of emotions does He feel? Disappointment? Anger? Discouragement?

In the Bible we read about God having all sorts of reactions to humankind's absurd behavior. He even expresses regret for having extended His love to such ungrateful creatures as we men and women can sometimes be. But there's one emotion God never feels. Nothing makes Him feel guilty or have a sense of "I guess I've failed with this child."

Our heavenly Father has done a comprehensive job of providing everything we need to be obedient children—sources of joy, pride, and glory for Him. He has furnished "everything necessary for life and godliness," says the Scripture. Nothing has been omitted from our provisions; we children of God have the wherewithal to live worthwhile and wholesome lives. He knows He's done His best, and that the rest (the choices we make) is completely up to us.

In light of the generosity our heavenly Father extends to us (and the way we sometimes refuse to appreciate it), it's no wonder that God understands what we parents feel! Some of us have given our very best to our own children. And although it may have seemed inadequate from their point of view, we did what we could for them. We tried. We've won a few and lost a few. And we've given the rest to God.

So why do we feel guilty?

Good question. Columnist Erma Bombeck was right: "Guilt is the gift that keeps on giving." Once we begin to nurse our guilt, it takes on a life of its own. We feed it with regrets and water it with tears. And how it thrives! We label ourselves as "malfunctioning" moms and "failures" as fathers, and we mourn our "dysfunctional" homes.

Why do we do it to ourselves? Is guilt our way of paying penance? Are we worshipping at the shrine of perpetual regret? The bad news is that there is nothing any one of us can do to pay for our sins. The good news is that the account is already closed; the price for our sins was paid on Calvary.

Here's another prescription—when we feel pinches and twinges of guilt, generously apply this Scripture as needed:

> If our heart condemn us, God is greater than our heart.
>
> 1 John 3:20

Instead of listening to accusing inner voices, let's remember the words of Jesus, who said, "My yoke is easy, and my burden is light."

God has forgiven us, and it's up to us to receive His pardon and forgive ourselves. But that raises another question. Does God forgive our kids the way He's forgiven us? Can He restore them to relationship the way He's restored us? Obviously, the answer to both questions is yes. Yet sometimes we act like our children's actions have made it impossible for them ever again to find the will of God for their lives.

Somehow I can't quite imagine God the Father pacing the heavenly corridor, wiping His brow, and fretting, "I can't believe he did that! That incident really caught me off

guard . . . it came out of left field. I don't know what to
do. He is only a teen-ager, and now my entire plan for him
is sabotaged. My hands are tied. . . . I'm so frustrated!"

Not to worry, friend. No matter what our failures as
parents, no matter how severe the prodigal syndrome in
our children's lives, be assured that there is no bad habit,
no incident, no accident, no disappointment, and no decision that can permanently prevent anyone from fulfilling
God's ultimate purpose. God's plan for the life of your
prodigal can be restored. There is every reason to believe
that God can put life's pieces back together, creating a picture even better than before. God is able to make—to mas-
sage, to manipulate, to maneuver—everything in our past
to work together for our good. Can we expect Him to do
less for our kids? In *Sitting by My Laughing Fire,* Ruth Graham writes,

> I think it harder,
> Lord, to cast
> the cares of those I love
> on You,
> than to cast mine.
> We, growing older,
> learn at last
> that You are merciful and kind.
> Not one time
> have You failed me,
> Lord—
> why fear that You'll
> fail mine?

We Can Bless and Be Blessed

I have always enjoyed performing in musical comedies.
When I was playing the role of Golda in a production of
Fiddler on the Roof, I noticed something interesting in the

script. As the children of Reb Tevye grew up, they continually challenged their father. And once they were grown, they no longer asked him to sanction their conduct. His oldest daughter, wanting to marry, finally blurted out to him, "Papa, we are not asking for your permission; but we would like your blessing."

Years ago Hal and his father experienced a theological separation creating a breach in the family. Basically, the elder Ezell was right, but Hal didn't know it at the time. After a number of years my husband began to try to heal the breach. One Sunday he went to his father and said, "Dad, I would like your blessing."

Dad had been a pastor for decades, and in the very same way he had blessed thousands of churchgoers before, he very soberly laid his hands on Hal's head and prayed for God's blessing. He showed no emotion. He shed no tears. But his gesture touched Hal and me deeply, and in a very real way. Any child can ask for a parental blessing, and even if he isn't as moved by it as we were, Hal and I believe that it makes a difference.

And we should offer our blessing to our children. We must find a way to bless them in spite of their behavior, just as our heavenly Father blesses us in spite of ours. After all, we don't have to agree with or be proud of our sons and daughters to love them.

Although God is not always a proud dad, somehow His love continues to flow. Jesus is saying to us, "Love one another as I have loved you." And God loved us way before we were lovable commodities! He didn't just decide to love us when we got humble; He didn't wait until we were begging for forgiveness either. But when we were "dead in trespasses and sins" He was extending His hand to us. Now He is speaking to us troubled parents when He tells us to teach them to do the things He taught us, "and, lo, I am with you always" (Matt. 28:20).

We Can Be Free of Anxiety

We've talked about burdens of guilt, but there are some other heavy loads that can also weigh us down. Maybe you've forgiven your children and have extended your blessing to them. But are you still carrying around undue anxiety on their behalf? Look at it this way, of all the things you've worried about with regard to your sons and daughters, how many have come to pass? And of the things that *have* gone wrong, what have you ever changed by worrying? Consider the wisdom reflected in a conversation between Corrie ten Boom and her aging Papa.

As a young girl in Holland during World War II, Corrie was anxious and fretting about how she could handle a Nazi invasion should the storm troopers arrive in her little town. To ease her troubled mind, her Papa asked her, "Corrie, when I take you to the train station, when do I give you the ticket for the train?"

"Just as the train is arriving," responded the puzzled daughter.

"Ah," Papa sighed, "And so will God also!"

Corrie's stories about God's grace in the midst of the Nazi holocaust speak volumes about His day-by-day, moment-by-moment provision. And we can be sure that each of us will be given the "grace ticket" at the time we need it, and probably not a moment before.

Anna Hayford, wife of Dr. Jack Hayford related, "Great comfort, and sense of peace, came to me with the sudden realization that not only does God care for our children, but that He intimately cares about us struggling parents as well; let's not forget that!"

A popular song says, "Don't worry . . . be happy." A more Biblical way of saying that is, "be anxious for nothing," committing everything to God in prayer, and trusting that "He is able to keep" the child we commit to Him.

> AND YOU CAN ALSO BE VERY SURE
> GOD WILL RESCUE THE CHILDREN
> OF THE GODLY (PROV. 11:21 TLB)

And no matter what happens, remember what God's Word tells us about Daniel and his friends after they were thrown into the Babylonian king's fiery furnace. There were "four men . . . walking in the midst of the fire . . . and the form of the fourth is like the Son of God" (Dan. 3:25). Jesus is with you, and although the flames surround you, blazing wildly and dangerously, you will not be burned by them.

We Can Pray without Ceasing

There's not much point in discussing patience—by now most of us have heard more than enough about "waiting on the Lord." Waiting is simply exercising faith—stretching our confidence and trust. While the time passes, we needn't be idle, paralyzed by hopeless resignation. It's time we activated our spirits by persistently asking, seeking, and knocking in prayer. Are our kids hopeless? Not as long as we stay on our knees before the throne of God, kindling the fire of hope for them.

Consider the words of John White in *Parents in Pain:*

> We must go to God with our problems and wait in His presence. We are to express our concerns fully and to tell Him of our bewilderment. We are to tell Him, too, that we know He hears and that we cannot understand what is happening.
>
> God never mocks people who approach Him in this way. He is patient and gentle, and He takes His time. Occasionally He may clarify matters quickly, but more often the process is slow. He wants to teach us

about Himself. The very problems we bring to Him serve as the basis of a lesson, a lesson through which we will be changed, our view of Him will become larger and the goal we are to seek for our children will be made clearer.

Author Oswald Chambers puts it this way: "Faith is not intelligent understanding, but a deliberate commitment to a Person where I see no way." No way for your child? You don't have to see the how, or the when, or the means by which they can have their lives changed.

We Can Trust the Great Physician's Prescriptions

Parents in pain have every reason to become parents in recovery! And in order to recover, we are going to have to look after ourselves, avoiding negative influences, and reaching out for more positive support. Although we confess we haven't yet learned the secret to loving unconditionally, we are working toward being slow to anger and quick to forgive. We are operating on the assumption that, with God as our example, we will never forsake our offspring.

And so the next time the feeling of parental inadequacy grips you like a chronic malady, remember these reliable remedies:

1. This child was God's idea.
2. This child holds the key to his own happiness.
3. A parent is responsible TO not FOR the child.
4. The Prodigal Syndrome isn't all that unlikely.
5. Wisdom says "allow them to reap what they sow."
6. Learn to let go . . . and take hold!

Let's take our medicine to activate healing, and ingest the tonics we need to ensure endurance. We are aggressively assaulting a crippling virus that attacks the soul with guilt and condemnation. We're injecting into our lives some spiritual nutrients which will enable us to be vigorous, healthy survivors of our parenting experience. And we're taking into our hearts and minds the following remedies from the Great Physician, which will bring relief and restoration to every parent's aching heart.

Angry?

> Be ye angry, and sin not: let not the sun go down upon your wrath. Neither give place to the devil.
> > Ephesians 4:26–27

> Who, when he [Jesus] was reviled, reviled not again; when he suffered, he threatened not; but committed himself to him that judgeth righteously.
> > 1 Peter 2:23

> Let all bitterness, and wrath, and anger, and clamour, and evil speaking, be put away from you.
> > Ephesians 4:31

> Lest any root of bitterness springing up trouble you, and thereby many be defiled.
> > Hebrews 12:15

Heartbroken?

> Don't worry about anything; instead, pray about everything; tell God your needs and don't forget to thank him for his answers. If you do this you will experience God's peace, which is far more wonderful than the human mind can understand. His peace will

keep your thoughts and your hearts quiet and at rest
as you trust in Christ Jesus.

Philippans 4:6–7 TLB

Afraid?

Fear not, for I am with you. Do not be dismayed.
I am your God. I will strengthen you; I will help you;
I will uphold you with my victorious right hand.

Isaiah 41:10 TLB

For God hath not given us the spirit of fear; but
of power, and of love, and of a sound mind.

2 Timothy 1:7

Feeling Forgotten?

Can a woman forget her suckling child, that she
should not have compassion on the son of her womb?
yea, they may forget, yet I will not forget thee. Behold, I have graven thee upon the palms of my hands.

Isaiah 49:15–16

Cast not away therefore your confidence, which
hath great recompence of reward.

Hebrews 10:35

The promise is for you and your children and
for all who are far off—for all whom the Lord our God
will call.

Acts 2:39 NIV

I will pour out my Spirit on your offspring,
and my blessing on your descendants.

Isaiah 44:3 NIV

Praying for a Prodigal?

And he that was dead sat up, and began to
speak. And he [Jesus] delivered him to his mother.

Luke 7:15

For with God nothing shall be impossible.
                                    Luke 1:37

And behold, a Canaanite woman from that region came out and cried, "Have mercy on me, O Lord, Son of David; my daughter is severely possessed by a demon." . . . "even the dogs eat the crumbs that fall from their master's table." Then Jesus answered her, "O woman, great is your faith! Be it done for you as you desire."
                        Matthew 15:22, 27–28 RSV

He will deliver even one who is not innocent,
    who will be delivered through the
    cleanness of your hands.
                                    Job 22:30 NIV

Single Parent?

He is a father to the fatherless.
                                Psalm 68:5 TLB

Thy father and thy mother shall be glad, and she that bare thee shall rejoice.
                                Proverbs 23:25

Feeling Cut Off from God?

For I am convinced that nothing can ever separate us from his love. Death can't, and life can't. The angels won't, and all the powers of hell itself cannot keep God's love away. Our fears for today, our worries about tomorrow, or where we are—high above the sky, or in the deepest ocean—nothing will ever be able to separate us from the love of God demonstrated by our Lord Jesus Christ when he died for us.
                            Romans 8:38–39 TLB

If I make my bed in hell, behold, thou art there. . . . Even there shall thy hand lead me.

Psalm 139:8, 10

Weak in Faith?

And blessed is she that believed: for there shall be a performance of those things which were told her from the Lord.

Luke 1:45

For the scripture saith, Whosoever believeth on him [Jesus] shall not be ashamed.

Romans 10:11

Have not I commanded thee? Be strong and of a good courage; be not afraid, neither be thou dismayed: for the LORD thy God is with thee whithersoever thou goest.

Joshua 1:9

Now faith is the substance of things hoped for, the evidence of things not seen.

Hebrews 11:1

Seeking Truth?

I have no greater joy than to hear that my children walk in truth.

3 John 1:4

And ye shall know the truth, and the truth shall make you free.

John 8:32

If the Son therefore shall make you free, ye shall be free indeed.

John 8:36

There is therefore now no condemnation to them which are in Christ Jesus.

Romans 8:1

Unloved as a Mom?

Her children arise up, and call her
  blessed. . . .
Give her of the fruit of her hands; and let her
  own works praise her in the gates.
                              Proverbs 31:28, 31

Those who sow tears shall weep joy.
                              Psalm 126:5 TLB

All your sons will be taught by the LORD,
  and great will be your children's peace.
                              Isaiah 54:13 NIV

Heavily Burdened?

Come unto me, all ye that labour and are heavy
laden, and I will give you rest.

Take my yoke upon you, and learn of me; for I
am meek and lowly in heart: and ye shall find rest
unto your souls.

For my yoke is easy, and my burden is light.
                              Matthew 11:28–30

Cast thy burden upon the LORD, and he shall sus-
tain thee: he shall never suffer the righteous to be
moved.
                              Psalm 55:22

Feeling Discontented?

And if God cares so wonderfully for flowers that
are here today and gone tomorrow, won't he more
surely care for you, O men of little faith?

So don't be anxious about tomorrow. God will
take care of your tomorrow too. Live one day at a time.
                              Matthew 6:30, 34 TLB

But seek ye first the kingdom of God, and his righteousness; and these things shall be added unto you.

Matthew 6:33

Let your conversation be without covetousness; and be content with such things as ye have; for he hath said, I will never leave thee, nor forsake thee.

So that we may boldly say, "The Lord is my helper; and I will not fear what man shall do unto me.

Hebrews 13:5–6

Ready to Give Up?

Be not slothful, but followers of them who through faith and patience inherit the promises.

Hebrews 6:12

A Final Word . . .

And let us not be weary in well doing: for in due season we shall reap, if we faint not.

Galatians 6:9